The People's Bible Teachings

LORD'S SUPPER

The Lamb's High Feast

Arnold J. Koelpin

NORTHWESTERN PUBLISHING HOUSE
Milwaukee, Wisconsin

Library of Congress Control Number: 2006923945
Northwestern Publishing House
1250 N. 113th St., Milwaukee, WI 53226-3284
www.nph.net
© 2007 by Northwestern Publishing House
Published 2007
Printed in the United States of America
ISBN 978-0-8100-1981-2

Table of Contents

Editor's Preface

The People's Bible Teachings is a series of books on all of the main doctrinal teachings of the Bible.

Following the pattern set by The People's Bible series, these books are written especially for laypeople. Theological terms, when used, are explained in everyday language so that people can understand them. The authors show how Christian doctrine is drawn directly from clear passages of Scripture and then how those doctrines apply to people's faith and life. Most importantly, these books show how every teaching of Scripture points to Christ, our only Savior.

The authors of The People's Bible Teachings are parish pastors and professors who have had years of experience teaching the Bible. They are men of scholarship and practical insight.

We take this opportunity to express our gratitude to Professor Leroy Dobberstein of Wisconsin Lutheran Seminary, Mequon, Wisconsin, and Professor Thomas Nass of Martin Luther College, New Ulm, Minnesota, for serving as consultants for this series. Their insights and assistance have been invaluable.

We pray that the Lord will use these volumes to help his people grow in their faith, knowledge, and understanding of his saving teachings, which he has revealed to us in the Bible. To God alone be the glory.

Curtis A. Jahn
Series Editor

Introduction

We all experience defining moments in our lives. A defining moment such as giving birth to a child or a tragic accident gives special direction to our lives because of its consequences. We learn from experience how precious life is, how precious each day of our lives is.

A moment to remember

Two thousand years ago, God gave the world a moment to remember in Jerusalem, Palestine. There a defining moment in world history occurred. God aimed "to bring all things in heaven and on earth together under one head, even Christ" (Ephesians 1:10). God demonstrated this special moment in a most peculiar way when Jesus Christ was crucified on Calvary. God showed us his love by the death of his Son (John 3:16). In that fateful moment, a great exchange took place. God now gives us eternal life in exchange for eternal death because of what Jesus did for us.

We all know how crucial life is. We hang on to life as ivy clings to an oak. Battling diseases that end life sooner than expected knocks the joy out of life. Lost battles with our sinful cravings often end in broken health, broken homes, and broken hearts. Life turns sour. News of loved ones who die tragically shakes us to the bone and casts a shadow over life. Lurking behind these battles is the struggle between God and Satan for control of our lives (Genesis chapter 3).

But God changed all that forever when Christ came (Genesis 3:15). The decisive battle between life and death was fought on a cross. There, Jesus, the Son of the living God, battled Satan, the father of sin and death. It was a strange and dreadful fight when life and death struggled. But the victory remained with life (1 Corinthians 15:57). Christ rose victorious over death and brought life and immortality to light through that good news. The death and resurrection of Jesus is the defining moment for our lives and for the life of the whole world. In all history it is *the* moment to remember (Galatians 4:4,5).

The Lamb's high feast

Jesus saw to it that God's decisive moment would not be lost on us. Before he died, Jesus prepared a meal for his followers to celebrate life. He now invites us to participate in this meal. Scripture carefully records Christ's invitation in simple words:

> The Lord Jesus, on the night he was betrayed, took bread, and when he had given thanks, he broke it and said, *"Take and eat. This is my body which is given for you; do this in remembrance of me."* In the same way, after supper he took the cup, saying, *"Drink from it, all of you. This is the new covenant in my blood, poured out for you for the forgiveness of sins. Do this, whenever you drink it, in remembrance of me."* (From 1 Corinthians 11:23-25; Matthew 26:26-28; Mark 14:22-24; Luke 22:19,20)

At this Supper Jesus gives us his life-giving sacrifice in person. Different from the sacrificial lamb under God's old covenant with Israel, we now have Jesus as the Lamb who takes away the world's sins (John 1:29). What this means is the subject of this book. As we prepare to go to the Lord's Supper we naturally ask questions: Why should we celebrate Jesus' death with joy and thanksgiving? Why do we call his Supper a sacrament?

The key to understanding

In this book we want to answer such questions by sitting at Jesus' feet and listening to his Word. We learn best by listening—and also by observing two cautions as the apostle Paul counsels. First, we need not get caught up in senseless questions about God's ways (Isaiah 55:8). They only lead us further from God's truth (John 14:6). Questions are certainly part of learning and require explanations. But when questioning degenerates into arguing over God's ways, it is like fighting fire with fire. Senseless arguing only ignites more arguments and gives more heat than light (1 Timothy 1:3-7). Second, we need to be careful not to chat about God's Holy Word as casually as shoemakers talk about leather. We cannot mold God to our liking, try as we will. God's ways are not our ways. We cling to God's truth as he chooses to reveal it to us (Colossians chapters 1,2).

Our questions, therefore, need to stay focused. The key to understanding God's Word is Jesus Christ. He came to earth to show us his Father's will. As simple as it sounds, God comes to us in his Word; we do not come to him (Psalm 119). Life with God is life *from* God, not self-generated. On our own we only end up with make-believe gods, artificial gods, gods of our own creation (Romans 1:22-25; Jeremiah 10:3-15).

Contrary to our notions, true knowledge and worship of God does not end up in dull and lifeless ritual. Christians gather together in congregations to celebrate life—our life with God and our life from God. God gives, and we receive. God acts, and we react. We respond in joy and thanksgiving because of his life-giving promises. God's Word is gracious and good (Psalm 100). The time warp between times long past and life in the throbbing present does not change the importance of Jesus' invita-

tion to us—today or any day. God is eternally present
(Hebrews 13:8).

To learn about the Lord's Supper we take a seat at the
banquet table. There in full view stand God's gifts. We
hear his words before we taste and eat—words of promise
and joy. At the Lamb's high feast God gives us his gifts like
handouts from a gracious king to undeserving beggars.
God's great gift is his love for us in Christ. We can return
this love each passing day by serving and loving him with
open hearts and open hands. Christ's life of superior service moves us to imitate him, our Lord, in serving others.

> I come, O Savior, to your table,
>   For weak and weary is my soul;
> O Jesus, you alone are able
>   To satisfy and make me whole.
> Lord, may your body and your blood
>   Be for my soul the highest good!
>   (*Christian Worship* [CW] 310:1)

1

The Lord's Supper

"Take and eat; this is my body. . . . Drink from it, all of you. . . . poured out for many for the forgiveness of sins" (Matthew 26:26-28). Christians live from Christ's words (Matthew 4:4). Every day around the globe, in languages strange to one another, people from every nation communicate in these simple words. As they receive the Lord's Supper, they eat and drink in common. This festive meal is, as it was meant to be, God's people sharing God's gift of forgiveness.

But people generally understand the Lord's Supper only superficially. When pagan people first heard the phrases, "Take and eat; this is my body. . . . Drink from it, all of you. This is my blood," they thought they were listening to a weird cultic ritual. In response Christian leaders tried to explain the Supper in more understandable terms.

But explaining is not easy. When God meets people, a mystery unfolds beyond comprehension. God reveals himself to us in a strange way. He makes his *hidden* will known in the person and work of his Son, Jesus Christ. Only by faith can we understand what boggles our minds (1 Timothy 3:16). The key to understanding the Lord's Supper lies in hearing and trusting God's Word and promises. When Jesus says, "Take and eat; this is my body," he means exactly what he says. God's Spirit takes our minds captive, and God's Word captivates our understanding. Therefore, we do best to explain the Lord's Supper in the way that the Lord Jesus instituted it.

What is the Lord's Supper?

What is the Lord's Supper? Good question. Instead of looking inside our heads to find the answer, we turn to Jesus for explanation. We listen to his words and pray that his Spirit would enlighten our minds. The Bible records the Lord's Supper in four main accounts. Three evangelists—Matthew, Mark, and Luke—depict the meal as it happened. The apostle Paul, by contrast, summarizes the event.

All four records highlight Jesus' words, but each writer singles out different details. The three evangelists spell out the details of the original setting of the Jewish Passover. Paul skips over the Passover setting, undoubtedly because the gentile world that he served did not relate to Jewish festivals. The account of the apostle John (not printed here) is unique. It records extensive table conversation and the details of Judas' betrayal instead of Jesus' words instituting the meal.

Taken individually, Matthew and Mark give parallel accounts. The records of Luke and Paul are also much alike. But all four writers include the basics. Jesus takes bread, blesses it, breaks it, and says, *"This is my body."* Then after dinner he takes the cup and states, *"This is my blood of the new covenant."* Only Luke and Paul add Jesus' specific command to repeat the Supper from that time onward.

To begin this study it is helpful (and refreshing) to read the records aloud as found in the Holy Writings. By reading the ancient happenings we are able to go to the live setting. We picture details as if we were there, and we can compare records as we read. A quicker option might be to read just one of the three evangelists—Luke. Then compare his record with Paul's.

Matthew the evangelist (Matthew 26:17-30)

On the first day of the Feast of Unleavened Bread, the disciples came to Jesus and asked, "Where do you want us to make preparations for you to eat the Passover?"

He replied, "Go into the city to a certain man and tell him, 'The Teacher says: My appointed time is near. I am going to celebrate the Passover with my disciples at your house.'" So the disciples did as Jesus had directed them and prepared the Passover.

When evening came, Jesus was reclining at the table with the Twelve. And while they were eating, he said, "I tell you the truth, one of you will betray me." . . .

While they were eating, Jesus took bread, gave thanks and broke it, and gave it to his disciples, saying, "Take and eat; this is my body."

Then he took the cup, gave thanks and offered it to them, saying, "Drink from it, all of you. This is my blood of the covenant, which is poured out for many for the forgiveness of sins. I tell you, I will not drink of this fruit of the vine from now on until that day when I drink it anew with you in my Father's kingdom."

When they had sung a hymn, they went out to the Mount of Olives.

Mark the evangelist (Mark 14:12-26)

On the first day of the Feast of Unleavened Bread, when it was customary to sacrifice the Passover lamb, Jesus' disciples asked him, "Where do you want us to go and make preparations for you to eat the Passover?"

So he sent two of his disciples, telling them, "Go into the city, and a man carrying a jar of water will meet you. Follow him. Say to the owner of the house he enters, 'The Teacher asks: Where is my guest room, where I may eat the Passover with my disciples?' He will show you a large upper room, furnished and ready. Make preparations for us there."

The disciples left, went into the city and found things just as Jesus had told them. So they prepared the Passover.

When evening came, Jesus arrived with the Twelve. While they were reclining at the table eating, he said, "I tell you the truth, one of you will betray me—one who is eating with me." . . .

While they were eating, Jesus took bread, gave thanks and broke it, and gave it to his disciples, saying, "Take it; this is my body." Then he took the cup, gave thanks and offered it to them, and they all drank from it.

"This is my blood of the covenant, which is poured out for many," he said to them. "I tell you the truth, I will not drink again of the fruit of the vine until that day when I drink it anew in the kingdom of God."

When they had sung a hymn, they went out to the Mount of Olives.

Luke the evangelist (Luke 22:7-39)

Then came the day of Unleavened Bread on which the Passover lamb had to be sacrificed. Jesus sent Peter and John, saying, "Go and make preparations for us to eat the Passover."

"Where do you want us to prepare for it?" they asked.

He replied, "As you enter the city, a man carrying a jar of water will meet you. Follow him to the house that he enters, and say to the owner of the house, 'The Teacher asks: Where is the guest room, where I may eat the Passover with my disciples?' He will show you a large upper room, all furnished. Make preparations there."

They left and found things just as Jesus had told them. So they prepared the Passover.

When the hour came, Jesus and his apostles reclined at the table. And he said to them, "I have eagerly desired to eat this Passover with you before I suffer. For I tell you, I will not eat it again until it finds fulfillment in the kingdom of God."

After taking the cup, he gave thanks and said, "Take this and divide it among you. For I tell you I will not drink again of the fruit of the vine until the kingdom of God comes."

And he took bread, gave thanks and broke it, and gave it to them, saying, "This is my body given for you; do this in remembrance of me."

In the same way, after the supper he took the cup, saying, "This cup is the new covenant in my blood, which is poured out for you. But the hand of him who is going to betray me is with mine on the table. The Son of Man will go as it has been decreed, but woe to that man who betrays him." . . . Jesus went out as usual to the Mount of Olives.

Paul the apostle (1 Corinthians 11:23-29)

For I received from the Lord what I also passed on to you: The Lord Jesus, on the night he was betrayed, took bread, and when he had given thanks, he broke it and said, "This is my body, which is for you; do this in remembrance of me." In the same way, after supper he took the cup, saying, "This cup is the new covenant in my blood; do this, whenever you drink it, in remembrance of me." For whenever you eat this bread and drink this cup, you proclaim the Lord's death until he comes.

Therefore, whoever eats the bread or drinks the cup of the Lord in an unworthy manner will be guilty of sinning against the body and blood of the Lord. A man ought to examine himself before he eats of the bread and drinks of the cup. For anyone who eats and drinks without recognizing the body of the Lord eats and drinks judgment on himself.

The original setting

The changeover from the Passover to the Lord's Supper is critical for us to understand. Jesus indicates that the Passover meal is his final meal for a reason. He is eating the Passover with his disciples because he knows he is going to be condemned to death on the following day, the day we call Good Friday.

In some criminal systems, a person's last supper has been called the hangman's meal. It is eaten before one is put to death. But Jesus does not see this meal in that way. For him the meal is the way to life with God—for him and for us (Matthew 26:42). It is extremely important that his followers grasp the meal's meaning. At this final meal, Jesus turns the age-old Passover meal into a new and even more glorious feast. He shows by words and actions that this new meal is anchored in God's ancient prophetic ways, even as God's old covenant is fulfilled in the new covenant that Jesus has come to establish.

Before Jesus came, Old Testament believers had observed Passover rites for 14 centuries. But with Jesus' advent, the Passover had served God's purposes. The lamb of sacrifice prepared each spring according to Jewish custom was to be overshadowed by Jesus' sacrifice on the cross. In the Lord's Supper, Jesus himself is the Lamb. And he gives the Passover meal meaning.

It is good to know what happened at a Jewish Passover to appreciate what Jesus is doing at the Last Supper. The Passover festival is unique to Israel and deeply embedded in its national history. The Passover shows how the nation of Israel carried the promise of the Savior to all nations of the world (Genesis 12:1-3). The feast celebrates two things simultaneously: Israel's suffering and also its freedom.

Throughout the years the Israelite people have never lost sight of that unforgettable day—the day when God released Abraham's descendants from slavery in Egypt (Exodus 12:31-51). Passover is the Israelite people's independence day. In every Israelite household people recall how God freed their ancestors from bondage and enabled them to return to the Promised Land of Palestine. "Our land is from God!" they say with pride. Each year families rehearse details of the exodus from Egypt. They do not merely recall what happened; they bask in freedom's glory.

It helps to understand the typical Jewish Passover celebration to appreciate what happened at Jesus' last Passover.

Passover

Among God's people Passover (*pesach* in Hebrew, Exodus 12:1-30) was not an ordinary celebration. Law prescribed its activities. The ceremonial law of the Old Testament commanded its annual observance (Exodus 12:14). Later Jewish tradition added many details.

The Passover meal, never eaten alone, traditionally consisted of enough persons to consume a one-year-old lamb. Diners normally were seated during mealtime. Custom later dictated that a person recline at the Passover meal as a sign of freedom. "Slaves eat upright"—the saying went—"but people recline to show they have passed from slavery to freedom."

Everything that happened reflected the people's faith in the Lord God of Israel. Participants ate the meal in a state of ritual purity. This means that the persons who had bathed did not need to wash again, except their feet (John 13:10). But participation in festivities had limits. Foreigners, unless circumcised, could not join in the celebration (Exodus 12:43,48). Without circumcision they lacked the sign of the promise—and the understanding.

At mealtime, flat loaves of unleavened bread (*matzah*) called exodus bread stood on the table. When a father was asked, "What is the reason for the bread?" he simply replied, "Because the dough of our fathers did not have time to leaven when the King of kings revealed himself to them and redeemed them" (Exodus 13:6-10). Unleavened bread had a twofold meaning. It indicated the Israelites' haste in preparing to flee (Exodus 12:11). It also recalled the days of the exodus when the Israelites ate bread unleavened. "Bread of affliction," they called it, recalling the hardships that accompanied their flight to freedom (Deuteronomy 16:3). In this way the Feast of Unleavened Bread gave a solemn start to the Jewish sacred year (Deuteronomy 16:8).

The weeklong spring Feast of Unleavened Bread began with the celebration of Passover (Leviticus 23:4-8). Households in Israel recalled the day in Egypt when the Lord mercifully saved the firstborn from death. Lamb's blood smeared on the doorframe—a sign that the house-hold believed God's Word—spared those marked for death in the plague that struck Egypt. The centerpiece of Israel's national celebration, therefore, was the sacrifice of a lamb, an unblemished lamb (Exodus 12:1-11). Customs changed over time, but the sacrificial lamb stayed an essential ele-ment of worship. As long as the temple stood in Jerusalem, lambs were dutifully sacrificed. Today Jewish families do not sacrifice a lamb because the temple is gone. But they still put a roasted bone prominently on the Passover table to represent the Passover lamb.

Passover ritual

How did the Israelites celebrate the Passover in Jesus' day? We do not know exactly. Passover rites probably con-sisted of seven table elements served in a pleasant and informative meal. Worshipers decorated the table with the roasted lamb and unleavened bread. Next to these food items stood a ritual wine cup to be ceremonially filled four times. Wine was expensive and was normally served—watered down—only at festive meals. The table also displayed bitter herbs like wild lettuce or endive, two dishes containing vinegar and salt water, plus a tasty red mixture of nuts and figs, apples, and cinnamon.

Jewish law prescribed preparing the Passover (*paschal*) lamb. Lambs, selected in advance, normally were slaughtered on the temple grounds in the afternoon—a sight to behold! At a trumpet blast, the celebrants, with lambs in tow, rushed the gates of the temple court. Priests and Levites were waiting in two long lines. The Levites' duty was to slaughter the lambs and burn each animal's fat, kidneys, liver, and tail on the altar as a sacrifice to the Lord. Priests, in turn, caught the lamb's blood in gold or silver vessels and passed them down the line to the altar. There the blood was spilled on the altar as atonement for sin. In God's eyes the animal's lifeblood covered the people's sin, just as blood on the doorframe had done in Egypt (Exodus 12:7,12,13).

The offerer then carried the lamb's carcass, which was wrapped in the skin, back home where he roasted (or cooked) it over red-hot embers, taking special care not to break a bone (Exodus 12:46). At sunset the roasted lamb was set on the table, and the Passover feast began.

At mealtime

To this day, at Passover meals Jewish families orally rehearse the story of Passover. The sacred story unfolds as the meal progresses. Mealtime lasts for hours, accompanied at times by the father's spirited dance for joy. After sharing the first cup (the cup of sanctification), the head of the household dutifully explains the significance of the special food elements and answers any questions the children may have (Exodus 12:26,27). According to tradition, the father, as teacher, conducts the Passover in such a way as to excite his children's curiosity.

As the father tells the story of the Israelites' deliverance from Egypt, he interprets as he goes (Deuteronomy

26:5-11). The father's interpretation always highlights the meanings of three things: the Passover lamb, the unleavened bread, and the bitter herbs. The father says something like this: "The Passover lamb is here because God mercifully 'passed over' (*pasah*) the houses of our fathers in Egypt (Exodus 12:27). The unleavened bread is here because our fathers were released in haste from Egypt. The bitter herbs are here because the Egyptians embittered the lives of our fathers in Egypt (Exodus 1:14)."

After each person has broken a piece of bread off the flat round loaf, each dips the piece of bread (*matzah*) in the sauce and eats it. Meanwhile, a second piece of bread traditionally has already been hidden somewhere in the home. Like a game of hide-and-seek, later finding this piece represents receiving new life that was previously hidden from view. After drinking the second cup (the cup of deliverance), the family traditionally chants from the great Hallel, a psalm of praise from the Psalms (113,114). This hymn praises the Lord for his majesty and for his mercy on the lowly.

The diners then enjoy the meal, eating the lamb, herbs, bread, and sauce. As they drink the third ceremonial cup (the cup of blessing), they thank God as the giver of all good gifts, especially release from bondage. The family then sings the last part of the great Hallel from Psalms (115–118) and ends the meal on a note of thanksgiving. Drinking the fourth and final cup (the cup of the kingdom) signals that the celebration is done. At the close, all joyfully repeat the refrain from Psalm 136, "His love endures forever," praising the Lord of Israel as Creator and Redeemer. The unforgettable feast is over. Midnight then approaches.

Two days after the Passover, there is an afterglow to the celebration. Families recall that the exodus from Egypt eventually led to the Promised Land so rich in milk and honey—and to a new life of freedom. In remembrance they wave firstfruits from the fields before the Lord in joyful thanksgiving (Leviticus 23:9-14). But, best of all, they recall God's special promise that from that land Abraham's promised son was to come. Promised son and Promised Land were bound together. They were preludes to Abraham's great blessing, the coming of the Messiah—the Savior of nations (Genesis 12:2,3)—our Lord Jesus Christ.

The Lamb's high feast

Jesus ate his Last Supper in obedience to Passover law (Matthew 5:17). At mealtime he informed his disciples, "I tell you the truth, I will not drink again of the fruit of the vine until that day when I drink it anew in the kingdom of God" (Mark 14:25). Since that instance, God's people no longer need to celebrate the Passover in the old way. What Jesus, the Son of promise, fulfilled—*and this is key!*—he did not destroy. He transformed the Passover into an even more glorious meal. The old is past; the new has come!

The new Supper

Why did Jesus change the old festival? In our experience, changes normally occur as things develop through repeated cycles over time. Things that develop into new things commonly come around again in different forms. Whatever goes around comes around, as we say. For Jesus, however, the changeover was far more. In God's way, the change from Passover to Lord's Supper was a final fulfillment of previous prophecy. The apostle Paul explains the changeover: "Do not let anyone judge you by what you eat or drink, or with regard to a religious festival, a New Moon celebration or a Sabbath day. These are a *shadow* of the things that were to come; the *reality*, however, is found in Christ" (Colossians 2:16,17). When the real thing is present, its shadow loses its significance.

Three things, therefore, mark the new Passover as distinct. First, Jesus frees the meal from its old ceremonial restrictions. The new Supper has fewer ingredients. There is only the earthly material (bread/wine) and the heavenly material (Jesus' body/blood). The Lord's Supper is now a meal under God's new covenant (Luke 22:20). Second, the centerpiece of the new Supper is Jesus Christ himself. He is the Lamb of sacrifice. The priests' *sacrificial* functions drop because Jesus is the Lamb of God and assumes their place. The service that Jesus renders is vastly superior to the priests' work under the former covenant. Jesus' work need not be repeated again and again. His work stands once and for all time (Hebrews 1:1-4; 7:26,27).

Finally, when Jesus institutes the Lord's Supper, he openly and clearly reveals God's new will. Those who eat and drink his meal publicly "proclaim the Lord's death until he comes" (1 Corinthians 11:26). Jesus says as much. In serving the Passover cup, he specifically states, "This cup is the new covenant in my blood, which is poured out for you" (Luke 22:20). God's new covenant uniquely frees us through the holy and precious blood of his chosen Pascal Lamb (Matthew 26:28).

"In my blood"

All four Bible records highlight the critical importance of blood in the new covenant. People are understandably squeamish at the mention of blood. Bloodshed means end-ing life. In wartime so much blood is spilled that the mere mention of blood can make people sick. But blood is one of life's great realities. Blood is as vital to our faith-life as it is to our bodily life. In reality blood does not signify death but life. We speak of it as lifeblood. Death results when blood is shed. In the Old Testament, God pointedly emphasizes how precious blood is in his sight: "The life of a creature is in the blood" (Leviticus 17:11).

Today we try to identify scientifically the seat of life in human bodies. Is it in the brain? Is it in the heart? But God sees life residing in the blood (Genesis 9:5). The use of blood gave Old Testament sacrifices their meaning. Blood sacrifices carried a distinctly personal message. God specifically told his people, "I have given it [blood] to you to make *atonement* for yourselves on the altar; it is the blood that makes atonement for one's life" (Leviticus 17:11). In God's eyes, atonement is key to the use of blood. This insight helps us realize what Jesus means when he says, "Drink from it, all of you. This is my blood." Those cryptic words also beg a question: What does *atonement* mean?

An atoning sacrifice

Atonement has been explained as—with a play on words in English—what makes us *at-one* with God again. Being at-one with God indicates that our broken union with him is now thankfully patched up. The break with God comes to light every time we knowingly and willfully wrong our Maker and sin against the One who loves us and gives us life. The trail leads back to our original forefather, Adam (Genesis chapters 2,3). Consequently, sin inherited down the line continues to separate us from God forever and finally ends in eternal death (Genesis 5:3;

Romans 5:12-14). But Christ's atonement heals the breach, reunites us with God, and gives us a life without end.

Reunion with our Maker, however, does not come easy. Becoming at-one again with the holy God remains the greatest story ever told. It is the story of Jesus' work of redemption and reunion. Paul writes with pregnant words, "God was *reconciling* the world to himself in Christ, not counting men's sins against them" (2 Corinthians 5:19). The one who tears down the wall that separates us from God is none other than Mary's child, the Son of God (Matthew 1:20-25). By an act of apparent weakness, Christ Jesus died to *atone* for our sin. But his *atoning sacrifice* broke sin's barrier and removed the long-standing wall of separation (Ephesians 2:14-16). This message, proclaimed in Christian worship, harks back to Jewish worship life. Then as now, atonement has to do with a *great exchange* that takes place between God and us. What does this mean?

God's great exchange is the core of Christian worship and the centerpiece of Christian life. The exchange between God and us is a magnetic field around which Christian worship revolves. It shows how sinners become saints and prostitutes become brides of Christ (Ezekiel chapters 16 and 23). It leads us to praise God for all creation and moves us to genuine love and service in our daily lives (Romans 12:1,2).

This life-giving exchange between God and us takes place by an act—an act that the Bible calls *imputation* (Romans 4:8 KJV). The act of imputation is easy to visualize but hard to comprehend. In the Scriptures imputation visually shows how sinful persons come to be pure, just, and right in God's sight. Old Testament Israelites understood imputation because they saw it happen every day, graphically, in their daily worship life.

Focus in worship

God set the pattern for Israel's worship life immediately after the nation's exodus from Egypt (Exodus chapters 19–40). At a desert encampment near Mount Sinai God formally prescribed three things that would bind his people to him: the law, the priesthood, and the tabernacle. The law showed the Israelites God's way of life. Priests administered the law—its rules, regulations, and ceremonies—to keep God's way of life constantly before the people. The tabernacle was the central gathering place for Israelite worship. On its grounds God's great exchange took place each day.

Israelite worship life focused on the altar of sacrifice for good reason. At the altar God released people from guilt and declared them pure and righteous in his sight (Leviticus 6:1-7, for example). The exchange took place as priests performed animal sacrifices. The act of sacrificing reinforced the word of promise once given to the Hebrew patriarch Abraham. In a vivid ceremony, priests preenacted the coming of the promised Savior (Messiah). Support for God's promise of mercy was a special function of God's old covenant law.

Animal sacrifices were an important part of worship because they demonstrated the exchange in action. The ritual of sacrifice portrayed atonement. It let guilty people know how God removes guilt. From God's viewpoint, animal blood on the altar served as a covering for sin (Leviticus 16:14-16). By the sign language of bloody sacrifices, sin's scarlet red was cleansed and turned pure and white as snow (Isaiah 1:18). The atoning sacrifice reunited God and his people in a most peculiar way. God shifted people's guilt to the animal substitute. How was this done?

Shifting guilt

Originally, the language of imputation came from civil courts. *To impute* meant to charge someone with criminal acts in a court of law. A person's illegal acts were put on record and counted against him (Psalm 32:1,2; Romans 4:8). But in the court of divine law the scene is different. God charges people with more than civic misdeeds. He charges people with sin—wrongs against him, breaking the royal law of love, and rejecting his way of life (James 2:8). When God says, "Be holy, because I am holy" (Leviticus 11:45), he means every word. In God's eyes the sentence for breaking his holy law is clear and indisputable. For the crime of thumbing one's nose at God's holy ways the sentence reads, Death—once and for all time! (Romans 6:23). The guilty deserve the verdict.

But God does not forsake or abandon us. God loves what he created and acts to separate sin and death from our lives. Unasked, unforced, unearned—solely by his initiative—God mercifully transfers our death sentence to a substitute (Romans 5:15). At the Israelite altar the guilty person put his hands on an animal and, by God's direction, imputed his sins to the substitute. The animal, innocent of wrongdoings, then carried the burden of the person's guilt—and also sin's consequences (Romans 6:23). It was then put to death—its lifeblood spilled on the altar to save a sinner from the death sentence. God stayed the execution of the guilty person on account of the animal's substitutionary sacrifice and forgave the guilty in an act of pure love. The act of atonement, done by God's design and according to God's Word, is vital for life before God.

The action at the Israelite altar, therefore, was not the act of a bloodthirsty god who loves death. Atonement is anchored in God's promise. It prefigures the great exchange to come, brought about by the work of Jesus Christ. By God's promise the real exchange will eventually take place in a tabernacle not made by hands (Hebrews 9:11,12). By the death of Christ on Calvary's cross and the shedding of his blood—miracle of miracles!—God shifted our guilt to his Son once and for all time. Isaiah forecast this final transfer in simple words: "The LORD has laid on him the iniquity of us all" (Isaiah 53:6).

"Too easy?" we might ask. Then consider this. God's action meant that Jesus Christ take on the burden of the world's sin *in his body* and by his death remove the world's guilt (1 Peter 2:24). Since Christ came, the old Passover sacrifices are no longer needed. In the new Supper, the blood of Christ is our true substitute and the atoning sacrifice for our sins. Not death but life is the object of God's will. God raised Jesus to life again for our justification— and by this act brings us new life (Romans 4:22-25).

The chief difference between the Israelites' worship and Christian worship is clear. In the Israelites' worship the animal sacrifice *prefigures* the coming of Christ as the centerpiece of Christian worship. In the ancient way of worship like in the new, believers can trust God because his Word is "Faithful and True" (Revelation 19:11). Neither Israelites nor Christians invented this rite of passage to God. Both ways of worship are anchored in God's promise of salvation, as previous history clearly shows.

This good news of God's love for mankind was present and known to all ever since the beginning of time. God never made a secret of the exchange between him and his people. He made the original promise to Adam, the father of us all (Genesis 3:15). Later he gave specific details of his promise to Abraham (Genesis 12:2,3), and later still he confirmed the promise by setting up sacrificial laws through Moses. Even then the blood of lambs, bulls, or goats merely served as signposts pointing to the Savior's real sacrifice (Hebrews chapter 9).

God's Word and promise, therefore, make true worship completely different from pagan sacrifices. A quick review of the five steps in the sacrifices of the Israelites captures the difference. In the Mosaic Law, the ancient sacrifices were performed through human instruments, but essentially they remained God's work done by his command. Here's how:

Sacrifice under Israel's law (Leviticus 1:1-9)

Step 1: *Consecration of the animal.* The sinner selected an unblemished animal from the flock or herd and presented the animal to the priest for sacrifice. This action took place by God's design, and the animal was set aside (consecrated) for God's purposes.

Step 2: *Imputation of sins.* The one who offered the sacrifice pressed his hand firmly on the head of the sacrificial animal and imputed his sin onto it. By this action the animal was officially removed from the possession of the worshiper and devoted to God. The animal was God's appointed vehicle to bear the sinner's guilt. It was God's own sacrifice.

Step 3: *Death contended with life.* The priest slaughtered the animal, and it died. But the victory belonged to life, because, as God saw it, the animal's death was the means to obtain the blood for atonement.

Step 4: *Atonement by blood.* The streaming blood of the slaughtered animal was immediately caught in a basin and stirred by the priest's finger to prevent clotting. Blood is the sign of life. And the shed blood was used as clearly designated by God when he said, "For the life of a creature

is in the blood, and I have given it to you to make atonement for yourselves on the altar; it is the blood that makes
atonement for one's life" (Leviticus 17:11).

With Step 4 the exchange was done. The blood was rit-
ually sprinkled on the altar. In this way the animal's death
brought believers a divine guarantee of new life. By God's
design the animal's lifeblood was substituted for the death
that the lawbreakers deserved. Blood sprinkled on the
altar, or the mercy seat, in the tabernacle covered the sins
of the worshiper, just as a clean white cloth hides filth
from sight. The worshiper was freed from sin for the sake
of the substitute. He stood *justified* in God's court. He
trusted God's verdict to be true. This faith, according to
Christian confession, is *imputed* to us for righteousness
(Romans 3:21-26; 4:5).

> Step 5: *Dismissal in peace.* Burning the animal's fat and
> flesh ended the sacrifice. The pungent smell of burning
> parts created an odor that was pleasing to the Lord. That
> graphic expression indicates how God delights in faith-
> born sacrifices, just as God "smelled the pleasing aroma"
> of Noah's sacrifice after the flood (Genesis 8:21). Thus
> Israelite worship ended dramatically. Guilty lawbreakers
> were declared free. Sinners were sentenced, but not to
> death as they deserved. Their sentence was commuted to
> life—life with God eternally. They were dismissed and
> returned home in peace.

Because of God's atoning sacrifice for us, believers of all
ages can live in true fear and love of God. The Israelites
heard an early echo of the absolution now spoken in
Christian churches: "God, our heavenly Father, has been
merciful to us and has given his only Son to be the atoning sacrifice for our sins." In thanksgiving, Jewish believers
offered their hallels in songs of praise. Christians today

offer alleluias of thanksgiving. New Testament believers join with saints of the past in thanks and praise to God for his undeserved grace and unspeakable mercy.

The Lamb's feast

How does Old Testament ritual fit with Christian worship today? Didn't Jesus free us from Jewish law? Doesn't the letter to the Hebrews explain that Jesus did once-and-for-all-time what the Israelite priests needed to do every day (Hebrews 7:27; 9:12)? The answers are simple. Certainly Jesus did. Christ is the "end [fulfillment] of the law" so there may be righteousness for every person who believes (Romans 10:4). In the early church, pious people asked the same questions we do. Sadly, some replied in an awful manner. They jettisoned the whole Old Testament as obsolete. For them the bloodthirsty God of the Old Testament was out; they were in favor of the New Testament God of love. But they were wrong.

Jesus did not dismiss the old worship or the Passover as obsolete. And God does not change (James 1:17). He fills the old with a new meaning. The new is Jesus himself. No longer do Christians feed on Passover lambs, bitter herbs, and cups of wine. Today we feast on Jesus. But there is a major difference. In the new Supper, Jesus is both the gift and the giver. He is the priest and the victim. He is the host and the Lamb of sacrifice. Different from the old Passover meal, the Lamb's high feast is a heavenly Passover. And we are invited.

The visible Word

In order for our worship not to end up spiritually abstract, our Lord Jesus Christ established a distinct way for God's people to receive his love. Today we call God's way a *means of grace*, a way for God to show and give us his unique love. If the thought of feasting on Jesus in the Lord's Supper strikes us as strange, we need to revisit the tabernacle grounds. There the sight of blood sacrifices will jar us out of our dream world into God's world. It is the real world of sin and salvation—our sin and God's salvation.

After revisiting Mount Sinai in the desert we need to go immediately to Mount Calvary in Jerusalem. There we learn the hidden connection between these two mountains. On both mounts God promised to cover guilt with blood. But on Calvary God worked with Jesus' lifeblood. And Jesus is a person, not an animal. He is God in the flesh (John 1:14; 1 John 4:2). He is God's Word made visible (Colossians 1:15). He is the Lord God who came into the world from God the Father's side (John 1:18). The sight of Jesus dying on the cross leads us into the real world of God's love for us (John 3:16).

Jesus' death on the cross was not a matter of divine play-acting like an act of a superman. Love cost God the life of his Son. We are redeemed by "[God's] own blood," Paul reminds us (Acts 20:28). The same Christ Jesus by whom all life was created is also the "atoning sacrifice" for the world's sins (John 1:1-3; 1 John 2:1,2). There is a wholeness and completeness in Christ and his work that is superior to our way of thinking (Romans 8:33-36). Now worship of God centers on him because of all he has done to bring us to life again—a new life in the presence of God, a life that lasts forever (Colossians 3:3; 1 Corinthians 3:23). In his Supper, Jesus takes lawbreakers by the hands and leads them directly into God's holy place—to a place where no human being has ever gone (Hebrews 9:6-11).

In this holy place we learn to know God as he wants us to know him. Here at his heavenly banquet we face God himself. He still remains hidden to our eyes yet we see him through the person of Christ Jesus. The holy and invisible God is as personally present in the Supper as he was in Israel's tabernacle worship. But there remains a significant difference. In his Supper, God *reveals* his love to us by *hiding* it under Jesus' blood. God's Spirit gives us the privilege of peeking beneath the earthly covering (1 Corinthians 2:10-16). As one Christian commented: "In the Lord's Supper, God comes to us in his *most hidden* form, under cover, as it were, so that we can approach the holy God with no fear."

Have no fear, only faith! By faith we understand that in the Lord's Supper we are partaking of Jesus as the "Lamb of God, who takes away the sin of the world" (John 1:29). In his Supper we are worshiping the world's Savior on whom God laid "the iniquity of us all" (Isaiah 53:6). Jesus' Word and Jesus' work give meaning to our eating and drinking at the Lamb's high feast.

2

Why Do Christians Go to the Lord's Supper?

When Jesus instituted the Lord's Supper, he gave compelling reasons for its continuation. At the last Passover he set precedent for future meals by stating explicitly, "Do this, whenever you drink it, in remembrance of me" (1 Corinthians 11:25).

Reason 1: Jesus invites us

We attend the Lord's Supper, first of all, simply because Jesus invites us to "do this." If the greatest king that ever walked this earth would invite beggars to a free meal, beggars would be foolish to refuse. But in his Supper, Jesus invites us to receive infinitely more than food for the stomach. He offers a special gift—a guarantee of life with God. We eat food daily because we need food to sustain life. Yet life is more than food for the body (John 6:32-40). As a whole person, each of us also needs spiritual food to sustain life before God. What activates and energizes life from here to eternity comes from God. What does this mean?

Life under sin

God created us originally to be his life mates. He made us "in [his] image" or "in [his] likeness" (Genesis 1:26; Ephesians 4:24). As his special creation, we possessed his image, were righteous and holy as he is, and were able to face him without bad consciences. But we lost God's image (Colossians 3:9,10; Ephesians 4:22-24). When our original earthly father, Adam, defied God's ways and sinned against him, he separated himself, his family, and all his descendants from God. Born from Adam's sperm according to the course of nature, we follow Adam's ways and die his death. Adam's descendants bear the stamp of Adam's image, not God's. Like Adam, all his descendants end their lives on earth in the grave (Genesis 5:1-5).

Since Adam's separation, like his our great sins are pride and selfishness (James 4:6). We continually confuse God's Spirit and our spirits. We follow the dictates of our own spirits, not God's. This fatal exchange must be undone to be acceptable to God. It makes using the words *spiritual* and *spirituality* tricky and deceives us for good reason (1 John 4:1,2; 1 Corinthians 2:11-16). The tragic loss of God's Spirit makes our spiritual lives totally earthbound (Romans 8:1-17).

Consequently, we lack true reverence for God from the moment of conception in our mothers' wombs (Genesis

5:1-5; Romans 5:12-21). We live self-centered lives and
worship God by indulging in spiritual routines that are
self-generated. Surely we still have a sense of God, who is
invisible to our eyes yet powerfully present in his creation.
But we no longer know God's *love*. Our sense of the
Almighty only drives us to appease him by doing deeds of
our own making (Romans 1:18-32).

As a result, since Adam's fall, only two religions exist in
the world. One is the religion of *works*. The other is the
religion of *grace* (Romans 11:6). The *religion of works* pro-
ceeds from our own inner spirits. The *religion of grace* is a
gift revealed by God's Spirit (1 Corinthians 2:10). What
all world religions hold in common, except for true Christianity, is that they are self-generated works-religions.

Works-religions require our own spiritual efforts to
please God. Characteristically, these works are law bound
and produce law-bound attitudes. Works-religions, at their
best, merely follow the golden rule—offering rewards for
doing "good" or meting out punishment for doing "evil"
(Romans 3:9-20). Followers of works-religions inevitably
answer to conscience as their final authority (Romans
2:14,15). And they end up performing acts of self-
discipline to make things right in God's sight (Colossians
2:20-23). In this way people by nature justify themselves
and their actions, no matter how off the wall their acts
appear. Tragically, Satan uses the works-routine to divert
us from trusting God (Proverbs 3:5). Works-religions
make us self-righteous and place us in a struggle that ends
in a full, final, and eternal separation from God our Maker
(Romans 8:5-8).

Yet God remains God. Our Creator wants us to be his
own dear children. According to his good pleasure, he
wills that we be holy, because, as he says, "I, the LORD

your God, am holy" (Leviticus 19:2). He desires that we
love him wholeheartedly, constantly, and consistently
(Deuteronomy 6:5; 13:3). No halfway or partial love will
do. With God it is all or nothing (James 2:10). That is
what makes God be God. Unable to follow God's ways by
nature, we arrive at a dead end. We need true spiritual
food to energize our lives. And God provides it.

Life under Christ
   God's way of life is the religion of grace (Ephesians 2:5).
Grace-religion displays God's love for us by revealing how
God acts toward us in love. A teacher neatly summarized
the uniqueness of God's love this way: "God's love does
not find its object but rather creates it. Human love starts
with the object." On first reading, we find God's special
kind of love hard to grasp since it confronts us with the
mystery of God's love in Christ.
   We certainly can understand how human love starts
with an object. We love by attraction. We love something
because it attracts us, it pleases our senses, and it answers
our needs. In our experience, attraction and desire go
together. But God's love is totally different. His love is not
jump-started by outward attraction for good reason. The
almighty God created what he loves and, therefore, loves
what he created (Genesis 1:31). What God desires finds
its source in God's heart alone, not in the object of his
affection. He loves us merely because he loves us (1 John
4:10). God loves sinners not because they are beautiful.
On the contrary, they are beautiful because he loves them.
The Bible calls such pure love *agape* (ah-GAH-pay).
   God demonstrates agape love by giving us gifts. First of
all, he gives us the gift of life itself—his creative love.
Then because of sin he gives us the gift of his Son to

extend our lives into eternity in his presence—his redemptive love (John 3:16). And finally he gives sinners the gift of his Spirit to renew life with him now and sustain it forever—his sanctifying love (2 Corinthians 3:6). Biblically speaking, God's love for sinful people is known as grace (Ephesians 2:8). It was grace that moved Jesus to become our helper in our times of need, to remove our guilt before God, to love the unlovely, and to make us heirs of eternal life. Such unselfish love makes God's gift of grace all the more amazing.

Jesus chooses to give us this amazing gift of grace in the Lord's Supper. He invites us to the table and offers all comers an unsolicited promise: "This is my blood of the covenant, which is poured out for many for the forgiveness of sins" (Matthew 26:28). Those who decline Christ's invitation or reject God's gift of grace in unbelief do so to their loss.

Reason 2: To receive an inheritance from the Lord

What specifically do people lose by not attending the Lord's Supper? They lose its benefits. They forego the special inheritance that Jesus gives us (John 3:17,18; Galatians 4:4-6). Each time we go to the meal we hear Jesus' *will* read aloud publicly. It is his legacy of love given to us to have and hold forever. At the table Jesus announced this divine legacy in simple and explicit terms. He said, "This cup is the *new covenant* in my blood" . . . "poured out for many *for the forgiveness of sins*" (Luke 22:20; Matthew 26:28).

What does Jesus mean by the *new* covenant? Jesus intended the new covenant to be a personal expression of God's will that would make God's former covenant with the Israelites obsolete. The old covenant, established at

Sinai with its commandments, rules, and regulations, was set aside because it was fulfilled. Like a new song, the new covenant celebrates the good news of God's unconditional forgiveness of sins. It was delivered—not by Moses, a human mediator—but by God in person and at God's chosen time (Jeremiah 31:31-34; Hebrews 9:15). Jesus used the term new covenant only once, at the time he instituted the Lord's Supper. He expressly called the Supper a "new covenant in my blood." All four biblical writers who put this subject on record include a similar statement of the new will (Luke 22:20; 1 Corinthians 11:25; Matthew 26:28; Mark 14:24).

The old covenant

Why did Jesus refer to the Lord's Supper as a *new* covenant? He meant to place the new in contrast to the old covenant. The new and the old differ primarily in God's timing and substantially in the persons involved (Galatians 4:4-6; Ephesians 1:9,10). Historically, the old covenant focused on God's ancient promises to mankind and the sworn oaths to the Israelites made to and through humans (Acts chapter 7; Hebrews 6:13-18). The new covenant, in contrast, focuses on Jesus as God's Son and the promised Messiah (Hebrews 9:15).

Prior covenants had been made with select people in anticipation of the time of the promised Savior. By contrast, the new covenant guarantees forgiveness and reconciliation with God, no longer by *promising* a Savior-Redeemer but by the Redeemer himself. This time God has acted in the person of his Son. Prior promises have given way to God's new dealings with us in Christ, who fully reveals God's will for us. Previous prophecies had been mere beacon lights in a dark world (Isaiah 60:1-3). Prophecies and promises now yield to Christ, the Light of the world (John 8:12). He is God from God, Light from light, true God from true God (John 1:6-9,18). Nothing needs to be added to God's new will. To do so would be like lighting a match to see the sun. This time God's work of redemption is complete, free, and done with finality—once and for all—as Jesus' dying words on the cross clearly tell us: "It is finished" (John 19:30).

In the Supper, God's new covenant is ready for its final earthly application. By this new covenant God atones for sin and obtains forgiveness of sins through his Son (Hebrews 9:15). Just as God's new covenant lies concealed in the old, the old covenant is revealed in the new. God clearly makes his will known in Jesus Christ. And he sets his new covenant in the form of a *testament* that accents his divine work perfected in his Son.

Society has always highly valued a person's estate and testamentary will. Every day people make legal wills. By engaging an attorney to draw up a will, they intend to pass a legacy to their chosen heirs. God has done the same. Initially he made his *basic will* known to Adam and Eve. He stated that he would regain custody over mankind by sending a woman's special birth-child to stop the rule of the evil one (Genesis 3:15). Later God revealed specific details of his will. He established a covenant with a Mesopotamian nomad, Abram, promising to make Abram's descendants into a great nation in a Promised Land. From this people and that place the Savior of nations was to come (Genesis 12:2,3). But just like a human will, God's testamentary will was merely a promissory note in lieu of death. It would not be finally executed until the will-maker died (Galatians 4:4; Hebrews 9:16-22).

The story of God's will does not end with Abraham. After Abraham's tribe became a nation and laid claim to the Land of Promise, God took further action. He added provisions—provisos that only a testator can make (Galatians 3:15-20). God made a special arrangement between himself and his people in the form of the Law, which was given through Moses as the go-between.

But the Law of Moses did not cancel God's previous will. The covenant God made with Abraham remained in force until the promised descendant came (Hebrews 10:1-10). Yet the addition of Mosaic Law put special conditions on Israel once it became a nation. The legal arrangement between God and his people, the Israelites, proved necessary for a reason (Galatians chapters 3 and 4). God had set Israel apart from other nations in the ancient world (Exodus 19:6; Isaiah 43:10; 44:1-3). And God's Law detailed how God's people were to live in God's presence. Mosaic Law exposed Israel's wayward ways and set boundaries to keep the nation from sinfully straying from God.

So the Law of Moses served a dual purpose (Galatians 3:19-25). As a *hedge*, the Law kept God's chosen people in bounds and separate from other nations. As a *tutor*, the Law trained God's children in God's way of life. Daily sacrifices and ceremonial rituals, like the Passover, let individuals know God's ways of love, mercy, and grace. Like children under parental supervision until maturity, the Israelites lived under the discipline of law. Abraham's heirs were duty-bound to obey God's covenant and live under its regulations and judgments (Deuteronomy 4:1).

The new covenant

At the proper time, however, God sent Jesus to fulfill God's original will (Galatians 3:23-25). The Son of *Man*, as Jesus preferred to call himself, did what no human being was capable of doing (Hebrews 4:15; 5:7-10). He obeyed the Law's demands freely, fulfilled each precept perfectly, and established the new covenant fully. He fulfilled God's will even to the point of bloodshed on a cross. Now it was the time for Jesus to distribute God's inheritance. At Passover he extended the wine-filled cup of blessing and declared to the heirs, "Drink from it, all of you. This cup is the *new covenant* in my blood, which is poured out for many for the forgiveness of sins." That moment was all-encompassing, never to be forgotten in future Christian celebrations and worship!

What makes the expression of Jesus' will at the Passover so special? In human terms, a will is a promise that a person draws up in anticipation of death. Normally a person's will consists of three parts: drawing up the formal legal will, stating the bequest, and naming the beneficiaries. Attorneys follow this simple procedure: (1) The maker draws up a will and has it witnessed or notarized to make it authentic. (2) The document describes and designates the bequest, the inheritance to be distributed. (3) The will specifically names the heirs or beneficiaries.

In his last will and testament—on the day before his death—Jesus followed the pattern. He himself was the testator. He made out his will in anticipation of his death by affirming, "This is my body given for you; . . . my blood, which is poured out for you." He then designated the bequest that his heirs are to receive the forgiveness of sins. And, finally, he named his heirs, or beneficiaries: "For you and for many."

Now we understand how significant and personal the Lord's Supper is. We are honored to be the heirs designate. As beneficiaries, we receive the premier gift of life with

God as an inheritance. God's old covenant is now finished, fulfilled, and made obsolete. And Jesus undersigned
the new covenant with his own blood. His blood validated
the will once and for all time without using animal sacrifices as death's signature (Hebrews 9:17-22; 10:8-10). This
Supper proclaims *the new will*—signed, sealed, and delivered in *Jesus'* blood.

Today in Christian congregations we can hear Jesus'
will and testament read aloud publicly. Each time we go to
the Lord's Table, God breaks the seal of his eternal will
(Revelation 5:6-10). And under the form of bread and
wine our Lord gives us his body and blood—a guarantee
that we are God's beneficiaries and heirs of salvation
(Romans 3:25; Hebrews 9:15).

Reason 3: To come into the presence of God

Receiving a bequest by means of a meal may strike us as
unusual. Inheritances normally come to us by the use of
legal papers. But God guarantees our inheritance in a more
personal way. He invites us to Supper. It is as if he were saying without a hint of frivolity: Eat, drink, and be merry!
This solemn occasion is at the same time joyous. By attending Jesus' feast, we can receive our inheritance and come
into God's presence without fear. How can this be?

God's presence

We need to recall that Jesus' presence on earth did not
end with death as ours do. It is true that Jesus ate the Last
Supper in anticipation of his death. But when he died,
death gave way to life. Jesus rose from death (1 Corinthians chapter 15). He left earth alive, only to return to his
heavenly Father (Acts 1:9-11). In leaving, however, the
Lord Jesus did not leave us without his presence. He

promises to be with us always until the world comes to an end. Today Mary's Son is present everywhere, and he fills heaven and earth with his presence (Matthew 28:20).

But God's presence in the Lord's Supper serves a specific purpose. Jesus chose to come to us under the form of bread and wine to assure us of God's forgiveness. His presence at the Lord's Table is a body/blood presence (we call it his sacramental presence). He said, "This is my body" and "This cup is the new covenant in my blood." By faith we cling to Christ's words as a *mystery* of God's grace.

A mystery

The Bible calls God's revelation in Christ a *mystery*—this word occurs frequently in the New Testament with reference to Christ (Ephesians 3:4; Colossians 4:3; 1 Timothy 3:16). In each case the mystery focuses on Christ's work of salvation and helps us understand Christ's presence in his Holy Supper. Christians are used to calling this mystery a sacrament. Ever since the Latin Bible used the term *sacramentum* for "mystery," Christians, particularly in the West, have called the Lord's Supper a sacrament.

In the Bible the apostle Paul identifies Jesus himself as *the* mystery (Colossians 2:2,3). He is the God-sent mystery, not in the sense of some myth or mystical truth represented by certain objects, like gods of pagan mystery religions. He is the mystery because he is truly God veiled in flesh. Far from merely representing God, Jesus is God in the flesh, the incarnate deity (John 1:1-14).

The mystery of God at work on earth unfolds in Jesus' life, as the gospels record. In a hymn dedicated to Christ, Paul shows how his work on earth progresses in our lives. "Beyond all question, the *mystery of godliness* is great," Paul states as a matter of fact. And then he explains the mys-

tery of Jesus' work in sequence through all-embracing
phrases: "He appeared in a body, was vindicated by the
Spirit, was seen by angels, was preached among the
nations, was believed on in the world, was taken up in
glory" (1 Timothy 3:16).

God wisely chose to reveal himself in a manner
unknown to the world (1 Corinthians 2:7-10). If only
unbelievers and authorities of his day had recognized Jesus
for who he was, they would never have shed his blood. But
God's revelation of himself goes *beyond* human experience.
In our scientific world, something revealed is no longer
hidden. A butterfly *comes out* from the secrecy of its
cocoon to unfold its beauty. It *emerges* from its covering to
reveal radiance that was previously unseen.

But when God reveals himself, he reverses the order.
God goes into hiding. He covers his glory and majesty and
hides himself in flesh and blood. At Bethlehem and on
Calvary's cross, we see God's Son only as the Son of Man,
just as human as we are—just as weak and as subject to
death. Only by faith are we able to see that this man is
God undercover, God veiled in flesh, God and man in an
indescribable, indivisible, and eternal union (Matthew
16:16,17; Hebrews 11:1). Faith alone grasps the mystery of
God in Christ and comes to know the secret of God's work
on earth.

The meaning of a sacrament

Now we know a basic reason why Jesus instituted the
sacrament. He wants to strengthen our faith in God. His
Spirit enables us to look beneath the cover of flesh and to
see God's great mystery unfolding there—"God was *reconciling* the world to himself *in Christ*" (2 Corinthians 5:19).
Now by faith we gain the full impact of the prophet's

words: "Truly you are a God who hides himself, O God and Savior of Israel" (Isaiah 45:15).

But, to our utter amazement, God hides himself not once but often. As Creator, he is already concealed in his creation (Romans 1:20). Then as Redeemer, God entered his own creation and hid himself there for a reason. God joined the human race, took on human form, concealed his earthly presence, and died on a cross to save the world from itself (2 Corinthians 5:19). The news of salvation is the precious gospel of the glory and grace of God.

Then, at his departure from earth, the Savior revealed his love for us once more by hiding himself from sight again. It has been well said: "In the Lord's Supper Jesus Christ comes to us in his *most hidden* form." Hidden from sight but revealed in his Word, the Savior comes to us and announces quietly and clearly in simple and explicit words, "This is my body . . . my blood." Jesus is present at the meal, hidden under the form of bread and wine, to reveal to us the death benefits of his work on the cross.

We might harbor the hope that God would come to us directly and uncovered. Moses once asked to see God face-to-face, but God turned him down flat and explained why. God is holy; we are unholy. If God should come to us directly in full-blown glory, we would die. "No one may see me and live," God explains to all who hope to catch a glimpse of his majesty (Exodus 33:18-20). Instead God comes into *our* presence. He comes in lowliness, covers his holiness, conceals his glory, and lets us see him from the back, as it were. There we learn to know God as gracious and compassionate. But we can only see him from behind as he passes by in our history, in our time, in our space, in our place (Exodus 33:22; 34:6).

Seeing Christ on the cross is God's way of dealing with us. On the cross Christ carried out his legacy of love to be our Savior-Redeemer-King. When the ascending Lord left the earth, he left behind God's legacy in the same way that it came—*hidden in a mystery.* He wrapped his legacy of love in his Supper. It was his means of having us come into God's presence so that we can live before the holy God in holiness. Mary's Son promises to deal with us by coming to us in person. "Take and eat," he says simply and sincerely. "This is my body . . . which is . . . for many for the forgiveness of sins." By means of the sacrament, Jesus gives us his body and blood and thereby assures us of his *abiding* presence.

Reason 4: To celebrate life with God

Celebration of our life with God and life from God is the basic reason Christians gather for worship. The Christian church is a liturgical church for good reason. In its liturgy the Christian congregation worships God, who makes his presence known to us in his eternal Word (Exodus 20:24). Though unapproachable in majesty and might, God approaches us in Word and sacrament. In return we can approach him with offerings of praise and thanksgiving for all that he gives us (Psalm 141:2).

Jesus designates the Lord's Supper as a meeting place to come into his presence. The mandate for assembly reads simply, "Do this in remembrance of me." At the meeting place, as at a festive banquet hall, he offers us his body and blood to memorialize an act of love that changed the world forever. Christ not only smashed the barrier of sin that stands between God and us and forgives us but, most important, by his atoning sacrifice he gives us his righteousness as a gift (Romans 3:21-25).

Christians rejoice in God's forgiveness thankfully and proclaim it fervently. But sadly some forget an essential part of the message. Besides *taking away* our sins, God also *gives* us Christ's righteousness as a gift. This exchange—the gift of Christ's righteousness in exchange for our sin—makes our life in God's presence complete (Romans 3:21-24). God does not merely forgive sin and then let us go merrily on our own, but he gives us the gift of his righteousness to sanctify our daily lives and actions (Romans 5:15-17). Like an electric charge to a dead battery, Christ's righteousness energizes us to work the works of God in life (Romans 1:16,17; Ephesians 2:10). Without God's gracious gift, the message of the new covenant is truncated and God's holy gospel is falsified.

We go to the Lord's Table to receive this gift of God, strengthen our faith, and celebrate our life with God. God's presence in his Holy Supper as Savior and Redeemer renews us. It moves us to worship God in joyful thanksgiving. We are truly sinners in the hands of a gracious God!

3

How Do We Celebrate the Lord's Supper?

Jesus instituted the first Supper in a worship (liturgical) setting. The meal took place during the rites of Passover. Worship of God is never formless, and worship forms reflect the setting out of which they come. Even worship that claims to be unstructured is bound to forms, often superficial and self-generated like in pagan idol worship.

New Testament worship

The ancient people of Israel worshiped God according to rites God prescribed in the Torah. Priests followed the ceremonial laws recorded in Leviticus, the handy scroll for Israel's clergy to use as a directive. The festive Passover ceremony invariably included lamb's blood and unleavened bread. These two elements carried God's message of salvation. Both recalled God's release and promised freedom. God carefully prescribed each element of Old Testament worship to remind people constantly that life depends on him, the Lord and Maker of all (Genesis 2:7; Deuteronomy 30:20). In the Passover rite, the bread of release and the blood of atonement forecast the final redemption through the coming Savior (see chapter 1).

In changing the Passover to New Testament worship, Jesus followed Israelite worship structure but freed worship from ancient restrictions. Worship of God continued to be structured. But the new forms reflected the *new* covenant. Worship no longer focused on signs of a coming Savior but on the Savior himself. The former bread of release is now Jesus' body, and the blood of atonement is Jesus' blood.

In the changeover, Jesus specifically instructed his followers on how to celebrate the Lord's Supper in the Passover mode (Luke 22:14-20). According to the four biblical accounts, only two types of material make up the new meal—the earthly material (bread/wine) and the heavenly material (Jesus' body/blood). They are sacramentally united to make up the Lord's Supper. It is God's new way of bringing us his grace in a worship setting.

Words for worship

The words used at the Supper are clear and direct and are to be understood in their simple literal sense exactly as instituted. Jesus' mandated words, "Do this in remembrance of me," mean more than a worshipful recall or a mere recollection of something that happened once upon a time on a day we now call Maundy Thursday. They aim specifically at *doing* what Jesus instructed and *receiving* what Jesus was giving.

The mandate, "Do this in remembrance of me," includes precisely what we are to do to remember Jesus' death. We are to take bread and wine as Jesus said, "Take and eat; this is my body. . . . Drink from it, all of you. This is my blood of the covenant." Jesus' body and blood make the memorial meal of bread and wine a heavenly gift, uniting earthly and heavenly elements as God wills. The Lord's Supper is truly memorable because we receive not merely bread and wine. We receive the body and blood of the Lamb who died for the sins of the world. How can this be?

When we eat the bread and drink from the cup, Jesus is certainly asking us to take bread and wine into our mouths. But what the mouth receives is more than mere bread and wine. Jesus specifically indicates that we receive his body and blood. Paul explains that this union of bread/wine and body/blood is a mystery. He tells the Christians at Corinth, "The cup of blessing which we bless, is it not the communion of the blood of Christ? The bread which we break, is it not the communion of the body of Christ?" (1 Corinthians 10:16 NKJV).

In explaining the mystery, Paul does not claim that the bread itself changes into Jesus' body. Bread remains bread, wholly and distinct in itself. Jesus' body likewise remains the body of the ascended Lord, wholly and distinct in itself. But in the Lord's Supper, the bread is so united with Jesus' body that we receive him in a way that is as mysterious as Jesus' incarnation. What does this mean?

When Jesus informs us, "This is my body," he is using a particular way of speaking where two things are united without eliminating the plain sense of the words. For example, we may say about a red-hot iron, "This is hot."

This evidently refers to the iron that has all the qualities of an iron. The iron itself is distinct from its heat. Heat, likewise, has its own distinct qualities. But in a red-hot iron, iron and heat are united as one. They jointly share their distinct qualities, as we know too well when we tell a child not to touch a hot stove.

In a way far beyond human ability to illustrate or comprehend, Jesus reveals what happens in the Lord's Supper by his particular manner of speaking. In saying, "Take and eat; this is my body," Jesus means that his real human body is present wherever the Lord's Supper is celebrated. Human bodies by nature are limited to time and space. Yet Jesus is more than a human being; he is also God. In him "all the fullness of the Deity lives *in bodily form,*" as Paul testifies (Colossians 2:9).

When Jesus presents his body in his Supper, he does so as one person. We worship one Lord Jesus Christ and not two—one divine and the other human (1 John 4:2,3). The good news is that God became a human being, one of us. God openly revealed this glorious mystery at Jesus' birth from a virgin, at Jesus' death on the cross, and at Jesus' resurrection from a tomb. God spoke clearly about the incarnation of his Son at Jesus' baptism and transfiguration. At both places God claimed and proclaimed, "This is my Son, whom I love" (Matthew 3:17; 17:5). If the world had recognized God's secret wisdom in Christ, its rulers would never have crucified him (1 Corinthians 2:6-10).

Now the body of the crucified, resurrected, and ascended Lord is given to us at the Lord's Supper (1 Corinthians 15:44-49). When Jesus says, "This is my body," he assures us that he is present bodily under the form of bread and wine. He is there for us. He wants to give us our inheritance. The real presence of our Lord remains a mystery to our minds, and God's mysteries are grasped only by faith. Faith is like a God-given hand that holds on to mysteries revealed by God—great mysteries of life, such as the creation of the world; God's revelation of himself as Father, Son, and Holy Spirit; and Jesus' incarnation (1 Corinthians 4:1; 2:6-10; Hebrews 11:3).

Without these divine mysteries revealed in God's Word we would not need faith (Romans 10:17; 10:8-12). Without them we would be able to understand and comprehend God on our own terms. Then God would really be no greater than our minds—and we would be god. Then our belief systems would be products of our own devising and God would be a mere extension of our deepest desires (Genesis 3:4). But then we would be also self-deceived, and the world's great deception would go into fulfillment in our lives. All this could happen because Satan separated mankind from God in its desire to become "like God" (Genesis 3:5).

But we cannot put God in a box. Christians did not invent the Christian faith. The Creator did not call on us to atone for wrongs by making the ultimate sacrifice of our own children (Micah 6:7). We did not ask God to sacrifice his Son to right our wrongs. God chose to reveal his love to us in a way beyond our wildest imagination. He sent his Son to take on our flesh and blood and by his death be reconciled with us (John 3:16; 2 Corinthians 5:19). Take Christ from our faith and there would be nothing left, only our own strivings to be good and godlike.

But God's strong love for us freely moved him to give his own Son into death to right the wrongs that his Son never committed (2 Corinthians 5:21). God did not spare his own Son. In an act of unbelievable kindness, he gave up his Son for us all (Romans 8:32). Christians have consistently proclaimed this good news since the beginning of time in their worship of God (Genesis 3:15,20; 4:26). In Old Testament worship, a consecrated lamb served God's purposes. But in New Testament worship, the Lamb of sacrifice is Jesus. And the Lord's Supper is the Lamb's high feast. Jesus explicitly indicates that he himself set apart his body and blood at the table to bring us God's forgiveness won on the cross.

It would be confusing, therefore, to understand Jesus' words "This is my body" in a figurative way of speaking. Such an understanding would mean that the bread was merely a sign or symbol of his body. On occasion Jesus does speak of himself figuratively. When he says, "I am the light," "the gate," and "the vine," he is not speaking literally (John 9:5; 10:9; 15:5). Jesus is not a gate made of stone or wood. The gate illustration merely helps our minds' eyes to see him as "the Way" to enter into God's house (Acts 9:2). The figure of speech lies in the descriptive words like *gate, light,* and *vine*. These colorful words are illustrations that help us picture something vividly in our minds. The figure of speech lies in the illustration, not in the word that links the subject with the picture.

But Jesus' body is a real body, not a picture, an illustration, or a product of our faith. When Jesus says, "This is my body, which is for you," he is not talking in picture language about some spiritual, figurative body. He is referring to his real, true body—the body that hung on a cross and now comes to us in sacramental form. His words make this clear, and by faith we understand what defies our eyes.

Acts of worship

As important as are the words with which Jesus is giving his Supper, actions must follow. We celebrate the Lord's Supper rightly and properly by acting on Jesus' words. We go to the table, receive food for the soul in our mouths, and eat and drink at the banquet in a worshipful way. As invited guests, we partake of God's heavenly food to be edified, strengthened in faith, and bound by God's love.

Formally, the meal consists of basic acts carried out as part of the full action of worship. First, the meal is prepared according to Jesus' direction *(consecration)*, then the banquet food is served *(distribution)*, and then we partake of it *(reception)*. As we participate, we are strengthened in faith, and the benefits of Christ's work become ours. Beyond these formal acts the Supper is finished (Matthew 26:30). God's heavenly food serves his eternal purposes as richly as bread sustains daily life.

It is important to carry out *all the acts* of the Lord's Supper as Christ ordained. Otherwise, the Supper does not serve God's purposes as a sacrament. Merely to consecrate bread and wine without eating and drinking them fails to fulfill Christ's design. The Lord Jesus intended the blessed bread to be distributed, received, and eaten, not stored or carried about in worship. A good guideline to follow is that nothing has the character of a sacrament apart from the use for which Christ intended it.

Consecration

New Testament worship of God in his Supper begins with three distinct actions that take place together: (1) setting apart bread and wine for God's purposes *(separation)*, (2) placing God's blessing on this food by designating it for use in the Lord's Supper *(blessing)*, (3) publicly proclaiming the banquet food to be Christ's body and blood *(sacramental union)* (1 Corinthians 11:23-25). Taken together, these actions make up the consecration. By these acts worshipers know that they are receiving God's food for strengthening faith.

As at Passover, God is going into action. And the action takes place by God's design. We receive God's own sacrifice. His sacrifice, completed on Calvary, comes to us under a God-appointed form of bread and wine. The earthly food and drink is set aside for God's purposes. The sacrament, therefore, is essentially God's work. It is done through human hands, which are God's instruments. In it Jesus brings us the atonement, forgiveness, and reconciliation previously promised in Passover rites. But now Jesus' sacred blood eliminates the need to use animal blood for covering worshipers' sins (Hebrews 7:26-28).

Paul highlights the act of consecration when he writes about "the cup of blessing which we bless" (1 Corinthians 10:16 NASB). The "cup of blessing" harks back to the third cup offered during Passover, which was called the cup of blessing in later Jewish writings. Diners received this cup for a special reason. By drinking from it they gave thanks to God as the Giver of gifts, especially the gift of the Israelites' new life free from slavery. Families worshiped together by singing the great Hallel from the Psalms.

In the Lord's Supper, Jesus gives the pascal meal a new form. The exact order Jesus used when switching from old forms to new forms is not clear from the biblical account. The biblical records do not indicate specific words that Jesus used in blessing. But the Scriptures clearly indicate why Jesus consecrated the new meal. The former cup of blessing is now "the new covenant in my blood" (Luke 22:20). God's people can now thank God that the cup we drink is the "communion of the blood of Christ" and the bread we eat is the "communion of the body of Christ"

(1 Corinthians 10:16 NKJV). Set before us at the table is the mystery of God's love in the visible forms of bread and wine, a witness to his grace.

One act indispensable to consecration is a public proclamation of what is happening. Each Bible record shows that Christ sets this meal apart in word and action. He *"took bread . . . the cup"* (act of separation), and *"when he had given thanks"* (word of blessing), "he *broke it and said"* (act and word of public proclamation) (1 Corinthians 11:23-25). The words Jesus uses—"This is my body . . . my blood of the covenant, which is poured out for many for the forgiveness of sins"—show the importance of proclaiming God's Word publicly in consecration. God's Word, when added to the earthly element, makes it a sacrament, according to a definition used in the early Christian church (Augustine in Tract 80, quoted some 1100 years later in Luther's Large Catechism, Sacrament of the Altar, paragraph 10).

Whatever order we follow, we should not leave out Jesus' words of institution. When the Savior says, "Do this," there is urgency in his mandate. The news is so important that it needs public airing, like news flashes that hit TV screens. The good news, Paul states, is this: "Whenever you eat this bread and drink this cup, you *proclaim the Lord's death* until he comes" (1 Corinthians 11:26). The words of institution are meant to convey this death message—and its significance—to the audience.

But the words of consecration serve a purpose beyond proclamation. They make the goods news personal. The words aim at our hearts. They are meant *"for you,"* as Jesus says (Luke 22:19,20). The words encourage participants to come to the banquet table, trusting that their sins are forgiven for Jesus' sake. They assure each believer that the

Lord's Supper is what Jesus says it is and gives what Jesus promises. The sacrament is a gift from the banquet host. It assures us that his death blots out guilt before God. It extends God's forgiveness to downcast hearts. We can leave at peace.

Distribution

Gifts alone without the giver are bare, a poet observed. Gift-giving involves the giver and is an intimate act of sharing. When Israelites of old celebrated Passover, families shared God's gifts of special food. Eating it recalled how God released their forefathers from Egypt. Bittersweet memories were coupled with joy-filled acts of thanksgiving. Each part of the Israelites' memorial meal highlighted the constant care and the prophetic promises that the Lord God gave his people. The festival was a family's intimate time with God—a celebration of community, never to be forgotten.

In the Lord's Supper, Christians also intimately share in God's meal. Under the form of earthly food we receive the body and blood of God's only Son. Each part of the meal highlights the Lord's constant care for our bodies and lives. Each part points to Jesus' death to make us pure and holy in God's sight (Acts 20:28; 1 John 1:7) and to Jesus' crucifixion to spring us free from death and evil. The distribution of bread and wine brings the family of believers these benefits in a personal way. When we eat at the Lord's Table together, we are in the presence of God together. The feast is a Christian congregation's intimate time with God—a celebration of communion, never to be forgotten (1 Corinthians 11:26).

Distribution of God's gifts takes place in sequence. Jesus first distributed bread, then wine from a cup. At Passover,

God trained the Israelites in faith by using unleavened bread. Without leaven (yeast), bread is pure and quick to prepare. Eating it signified the haste of the Israelites' exodus and the hardship (Exodus 12:17-20). It kept God's promises before each diner's eyes, as did the traditional use of the cup filled with watered-down wine.

But Jesus' new meal, set free from Old Testament restrictions, does not focus on the makeup of bread and the cup (Matthew 26:29; Mark 14:25). Using bread is essential—whether leavened or unleavened, baked in loaves or wafers, made of oats, barley, wheat, corn, rice, or rye—provided one uses simple bread baked from flour and water (Matthew 26:26). The same holds true for the cup. Whether one uses white wine or red, watered-down wine or the juice of still unfermented grapes is not essential—provided that we drink of the "fruit of the vine" (Matthew 26:29; Mark 14:25; Luke 22:18). Christian churches today freely and almost uniformly follow the past practice of using unleavened bread and wine, primarily because of their historical significance and to honor Jesus' example.

Even distribution customs are not prescribed. To insist on breaking bread because Jesus broke bread off a loaf at the first Supper goes beyond Jesus' institution (Luke 22:19). Customs such as reclining at the meal, washing feet before eating, breaking off pieces from flat loaves instead of slicing, or lifting up hands to pray were meaningful practices in vogue at Jesus' time (Luke 22:14; John 13:2-5; 1 Timothy 2:8). But they are not essential in celebrating the Lord's Supper.

Only the formal actions of consecration, distribution, and reception are needed to fulfill the command and purpose of Jesus' meal. All else is done in Christian liberty. In matters of custom, Christians aim to act in love—fostering meaningful worship in form and beauty (Philippians 4:8) and seeking unity in worship without insisting on uniformity in every custom or ceremony (1 Corinthians 10:23-31). Insistence on only one way in matters of Christian freedom takes away freedom. Such action may call for a witness to those who take Christian liberty away by making custom into new ceremonial law (Colossians 2:16,17).

This freedom also applies to the words spoken at the time of distribution. In serving bread and wine, we can repeat words used previously in the consecration for several reasons. Repeating Jesus' words gives those who come to the meal personal assurance of the precious gift they are receiving. At the same time, repeating the words gives a public testimony of Christian faith in clear and unmistakable terms. But the words spoken at the distribution may vary.

Care is needed, however, because the word-formula used for distribution can mask a false understanding of the Supper. Using the words *"[Jesus] said, 'This is my body'"* looks good on the surface and can be taken rightly. But the words can be misleading, especially when some insist on this set wording to cover their notions. In the formula *"Jesus said,"* the words of distribution can have an ambiguous effect similar to the words Jesus spoke to the Roman governor before his crucifixion.

When Pilate asked Jesus if he was a king, Jesus truthfully answered, "I am a king" (John 18:37). Jewish opponents denied Jesus' kingship. Yet they were willing to let Jesus' claim to kingship stand for a reason. The legal record would read ambiguously, *"Jesus said, 'I am a king,'"* as if this were merely Jesus' claim but not really true (John 19:21). In the face of this equivocal wording, Christians later reworded Jesus' statement to reflect his meaning and to give a clear-cut testimony of their faith in him as King. Emphatically and unequivocally they stated, Jesus is really and truly a King, and he has come to save the world from sin (John 1:49; 12:13; 19:35; 1 Timothy 1:17; 6:13-16).

Similarly, Christians today may distribute the bread with words such as, "Take and eat. This is the *true* body of our Lord and Savior, Jesus Christ, given into death for your sins." Such a freely worded verbal witness leaves no doubt as to what guests at the table are receiving and why. Words true to Jesus' mandate publicly proclaim and openly profess what Jesus intended the people to know. In his Sacrament, the mystery of Christ is at work. All who participate in the Lamb's high feast must know that they are receiving the very body and blood of "the Lamb of God, who takes away the sin of the world" (John 1:29). Christians are celebrating their lives with God.

Reception

In the act of receiving the Lord's Supper, Christians likewise follow Christ's instructions. When Jesus says, "Take and eat" or "drink from it," he is giving more than an invitation to the table. He is also issuing a gracious command. He wants no one in attendance to leave without receiving both the bread and the wine. To receive bread alone is not the intent of Jesus' institution, nor should we change his loving mandate. To give guests only bread (body) without the cup falls short of Jesus' command, especially because Jesus attributes universality to the cup. He says, "Drink from it, *all of you*" (Matthew 26:27).

How Jesus' followers received the sacred food at the first Supper is not clear (Matthew 26:26,27). We do not know whether Jesus broke off pieces of the consecrated bread for each guest individually or distributed it in another fashion, or whether Jesus held the cup to each person's lips or passed the cup around. Essential for faith is the fact that Jesus distributed the bread and wine with the words of his new covenant. A single word from the mouth of God's Son is a powerful pledge of God's love for his creatures (Hebrews 1:1). Jesus speaks so that we might believe "and that by believing [we] may have life in his name" (John 20:31).

Believing God is the ultimate goal of worship because faith takes God at his Word. By faith we hold God to his Word and promises, as Jacob did when he wrestled with God and won (Genesis 32:28). Without faith we lose God's grace, mercy, and love for us. Without faith God loses his glory and majesty in our lives. There is no greater worship of God than to attribute majesty and glory, divinity and truth, wisdom and honor to the Lamb that was slain for us (Revelation 5:12,13). Jesus cares. He is the seeker, and we are the ones sought (Luke 19:10). The words from his mouth are living, true, and powerful, and they are able to accomplish what he pleases (Hebrews 4:12; Isaiah 55:11).

Precisely because the Lord's Supper is God's Word *to us*, we receive bread and wine in worshipful awe and reverence. We come into God's presence with the same respect that we do when his Word is preached. But there is a difference. In the Supper we receive God's blessings under visible signs. Our faith does not make God present. Only God's gracious Word and promise make the Supper what it is. Yet by receiving his Holy Sacrament, by faith we *secure* God's blessings won on the cross.

The sacrifice of Christ, sacramentally received, moves us to give God praise and thanks and to glorify his name. We bless his holy name because he blesses us. In view of

God's mercies, his Spirit leads us to offer our lives wholeheartedly to him in God-pleasing service. Paul calls this
kind of offering a "spiritual act of worship" (Romans 12:1).
In this way our worship comes full circle. "We love
because he first loved us" (1 John 4:19). And true love
means that with thanks "we walk in obedience to [God's]
commands" (2 John 6).

Acting in thanksgiving is a goal of the Lord's Supper.
Christians may refer to the Lord's Supper as the Eucharist
for good reason. When Jesus took the cup, he gave thanks
and called on God to bless the cup. In the Greek language, the word for giving thanks is *eucharist*
(*eucharistein*—oi-car-ist-INE in Luke 22:19; 1 Corinthians
11:24). Many Christians designate the Lord's Supper as
the Eucharist, meaning "thanksgiving."

Following Jesus' lead, we surround the Supper with
thanksgiving. At the beginning of the meal, Christians
call for God's blessing on his Supper. We lift our hearts
and offer the God of all creation thanks for his mighty
acts, especially for the salvation freely offered us in Christ
(Psalm 145). The Holy God is present at his Supper! The
blessing of salvation comes to us under the form of fruits of
the field—bread and wine—to be consecrated for our benefit. The gifts we receive at God's table are special gifts of
love, the very body and blood of our Lord and Savior,
Jesus the Christ. After receiving his life-sustaining gifts,
we reciprocate. We end the meal by offering him our
thanks for his salvation (1 John 4:19).

Offering praise is our way of thanking God for his
legacy of love. He has filled our hands and hearts with
good gifts and has united himself with us in intimate communion (1 Corinthians 10:17). We leave at peace. Like
Simeon, the seer of old, our eyes have seen God's salvation

prepared in the sight of all people, visibly and tangibly (Luke 2:29-32). The Lamb's high feast is at an end. We are dismissed with God's blessing.

4

How Does the Lord's Supper Serve the Church?

At the first Supper (though Jesus' last), our Lord indicated more than why and how Christians are to celebrate the new meal. He also mandated its continuation for a reason (Luke 22:19). After ascending to heaven, Jesus left this holy feast in place to help the church on earth in two specific ways. The Supper aims to serve as a visible, *outward sign* of God's grace to Christ's church. We might say it marks the church as present for all to see. At the same time, this holy meal also graphically puts God's stamp on believers and thus *seals* his love for us in unmistakable terms (1 Corinthians 11:26).

Marking the church

As a visible sign, the Lord's Supper outwardly marks Christian assemblies. This sign is a badge that identifies Christians in an unbelieving world (1 Corinthians 10:18-21). Other signs, such as prayer and persecution, can also indicate the church's presence in a given place. But the unmistakable and most distinctive signs of God's presence in the church, aside from preaching, are the Lord's Supper and Baptism. Both are visible to the eye because of the use of water and bread/wine. And both bear the distinctive Christian message. Like preaching, they serve to proclaim the gospel of God's love for us (1 Corinthians 11:26).

When pagan people observed early Christians at worship, they wondered what was going on in the assemblies. Their eyes saw only bread and wine being distributed with a promise: "Take and eat; this is my body. . . . Drink from it, all of you. This is my blood of the covenant, which is poured out for many for the forgiveness of sins." On hearing such words, they grasped at explanations. Nevertheless, these outward signs led unbelievers to recognize the Christian church for what Christ meant it to be: Believers using earth's elements in worship of God.

The meaning of church

From the Christian church's beginnings, believers gathered into congregations to hear the Christian gospel and to eat the Supper (Acts 2:42). The intimate relation between Sacrament and congregation highlights the meaning of the word *church*. Originally, people never used the expression *church* with reference to a building. As adherents of an outlawed religion, early Christians did not have permanent structures for worship as we know them today. Yet the first Christians were not without gathering places. They spoke of church as an assembly marked by Christ's presence in his Word wherever believers gathered (Acts 2:41; 11:22,26).

The call to assemble for worship in the Lord's presence gave new meaning to the everyday Greek word *ecclesia* (ek-lay-SEE-ah—in English *ecclesiastical*). In Greek society *ecclesia* meant a gathering of people summoned by the town crier. But among Christians the word came to mean a Christian assembly called to worship God. Wherever Christians gathered—whether in the open air, in a house, or in a cave—the assembly of believers was a *church*, and *church* meant nothing more than a believers' assembly (Galatians 1:2).

Believers called by God simply congregated around God's Word (Matthew 18:20; 28:18-20). At the gathering place, they preached, baptized, ate God's meal, and offered God prayers, praise, and thanks for what they received. In God-fearing reverence, they worshiped, they cared, and they shared (Acts 2:41-47). Their church was a Christian community, a communion of saints, so named because people held *in common* the Holy Communion—as the word itself suggests. In later years congregational leaders joined people and Sacrament into one. When distributing bread and wine, the leader announced to the assembly, "Holy things to holy people!"

Serving bread and wine at the assembly came to mark the Christian church visibly and to identify Christians uniquely. Ever since the first meal, the visible elements and the words of distribution mark Christian worship as distinct from other such ceremonies (1 Corinthians 11:14-33). Both Christian and non-Christian religions often involve ceremonial foods. But the similarity ends there. Failure to distinguish Christian signs from non-Christian ceremonies results in confusion. It happened at Corinth in Paul's day.

Some Corinthian Christians failed to grasp how eating pagan ceremonial food differed from the Christian Supper. As a result they threw the congregation into division by freely eating both idol food and the Lord's Supper (1 Corinthians 8:1-13). Food itself was not the problem. God gives food for eating, and it can be eaten freely. Even food dedicated to idols and sold on the open market does not make the food inedible for one simple reason: Idols do not really exist. They are mere make-believe gods, figments of people's imaginations, visual images made of natural forces (1 Corinthians 10:25,26; 8:4; Romans 1:22,23). Christians who understand true Christian freedom can, therefore, eat marketed food without offense and with a clear conscience, even food marked with a religious stamp (1 Corinthians 8:7,8; Acts 10:9-15).

But circumstances vary. The situation changes and becomes downright injurious to faith when Christians join non-Christians in their religious rites (1 Corinthians 10:27-29). In such cases ceremonial food becomes a critical element. Participation in another's religious rite gives a stamp of approval to that religion and hinders a clear testimony to the true and living God. Why is this so? If we join in fellowship with those that deny Jesus' saving work, we deny the very faith that his Supper aims to build. Such religious fellowship, getting together and rubbing elbows with other people in a public ceremony, is not an innocent practice. True worship remains worship of God in truth (John 8:31). And participation in other people's religious rites raises questions concerning what god we are honoring (John 5:22,23). By joining in worship we identify ourselves with that religion. How is this done?

Satan is up to his old tricks. He uses the intimacy of worship to deceive us by mimicking God's ways. Under the guise of religious ceremony, the evil one does what he did with dedicated food in the Garden of Eden (Genesis 3:5). He challenges God. He diverts us from following God's Word and promises. Subtly, Satan neutralizes our allegiance to Christ the Savior and simultaneously leads unbelievers to think that Christianity is just another religion on the marketplace. God uses the Lord's Supper, therefore, to mark the bounds of Christian fellowship. Participation in the Christian feast draws a line between the true Christian faith and all false religions (1 Corinthians 10:23-31).

The apostle Paul identifies this function of the Lord's Supper when he writes with unmistakable clarity, "The sacrifices of pagans are offered to demons, not to God. . . . You cannot drink the cup of the Lord and the cup of demons too; you cannot have a part in both the Lord's table and the table of demons" (1 Corinthians 10:20,21). The consequence of joining in worship with non-Christian religions and false ceremonies is enormous. In effect, such democratic action effectively erases the boundary line between idolatry and worship of the true God. It defies God's first requirement in worship: "You shall have no other gods before me" (Exodus 20:3). Specifically, it makes a mockery of the Christian confession on which the Lord's Supper is based. The apostle Paul says that this is the true Christian belief (creed): "For us there is but one God, the Father, from whom all things came and for whom we live; and there is but one Lord, Jesus Christ, through whom all things came and through whom we live" (1 Corinthians 8:6).

Undermining the church's faith in God by false fellowship eventually erodes the Christian testimony. It works to

destroy the true church—if that were possible (1 Kings
19:14-18). The Christian church, by definition, is *hidden*
to the natural eye (Luke 17:20). The true church is the
assembly of all believers throughout the world who hold
faith in the triune God *in their hearts*. It has been well said
that the line of division between church and non-church
is *faith* (Ephesians 2:8,9; Romans 11:6). And the seat of
faith is in the heart (Romans 10:10). Neither organiza-
tion, nor geography, nor race, nor hierarchy, nor country,
nor tribe defines the church or makes a person a member
of it. Faith alone sets the Christian church's bounds, just
as faith alone makes us righteous before God (Romans
1:17; 4:1-3).

Marks of the church

How then can we find the church since God alone can
see our hearts (1 Samuel 16:7; 2 Corinthians 5:12)? Does
such a *hidden church* virtually make the church unreal,
some ethereal thing floating in the air but nowhere to be
found? Not so! Thanks to God the church can be known
on earth. We can get to know the church by its outward
signs. The church is made visible by its signs. It is found
wherever believers assemble around the gospel and the
sacraments.

The true church is where one can hear God's Word
purely preached and receive the sacraments as God mandated their use (Matthew 28:18-20; 1 Corinthians
11:24,25). That is why social gatherings and social behavior are not clear and identifiable marks of the church.
Such a mere sociological understanding of the church is
foreign to the faith and fellowship of Christ's church. It
confuses people. All world religions have outward signs,
and their practitioners can seemingly outstrip Christians

when measured by observable disciplined behavior
(Romans 2:14,15).

But the church does not live by morals, by the knowledge and observance of God's law (Romans 2:12,13). Nor
does it live by religion, by lofty experiences of the divine,
or by an awareness of the mysteries of God (Romans
11:33-36). It lives solely by the forgiveness of sins (John
17:3; Philippians 3:8-11). Forgiveness of sins and Christ's
righteousness are the church's foundation, its focus, and its
main message (Acts 4:10-12). And Christ offers these
divine gifts freely in his Supper.

This means that Christian faith is not built on faith itself
or on a Christian's life of faith. In his infinite wisdom, God
wills that a Christian's life grows *out of* Christian faith,
even as a tree's fruit comes from the tree (Galatians 5:22-
26). In God's order of things, God's Word comes first, faith
follows, then come love and good works as fruits of faith.
God's Word and sacraments clearly mark the church's presence. And God's people gratefully receive his gracious signs
whenever they gather around his Word and sacraments to
worship him in true thanksgiving *(eucharist)*.

Despite the outward signs, the true church remains
hidden in a crowd of people. Believers live among false
Christians. In Christian assemblies, hypocrites are easily
disguised, like weeds growing in a wheat field (Matthew
13:24-30). But the presence of unbelievers does not cause
the church to disappear. Nor does a believer's faith create
the church, make God present, or make the sacraments
what they are. God's Word and sacraments alone establish
the Christian church. These marks remain powerful apart
from believers' faith or unbelievers' hypocrisy for good reason. Their power is from God (Isaiah 55:11; Romans
1:16). God alone builds his church and gives it a full iden-

tity. And he does so through means established by Christ and anchored in his Word.

Simply put, the one infallible sign of the church is the holy gospel of the Lord Jesus Christ (2 Timothy 1:8-10). Where Christ is present, the church is found. A special mark of Christ's gracious presence is his body and blood given to us to eat and drink. "Do this," he commands, "in remembrance of *me*."

Sealing God's gracious will

But the Supper serves an even more specific purpose within the Christian congregation. To believers, the Lord's body and blood is a *visible seal* of God's forgiveness under a specific form. At the Lord's Table, members of Christ's body of believers are joined with their Head in a union (Ephesians 4:15; 1 Corinthians 10:16,17). The seal of forgiveness guarantees the unity of Christ with his church and strengthens the bond of faith in God.

The chief function of the Lord's Supper, therefore, is to serve believers. God uses his Supper to strengthen our faith in him. Under the form of bread and wine, God acts to seal his gracious will toward us. He seals his *new* covenant with humankind by the blood of his Son (Hebrews 9:11-14). Similar to the function of a legal transaction, God signs, seals, and delivers his divine will. It is guaranteed and notarized with God's own blood and thus affects the life of the whole world (Hebrews 9:16-18).

Prior to the coming of Christ Jesus, God had sealed his covenant with Abraham with a distinct outward sign, the sign of circumcision (Genesis chapter 17; Exodus 4:25; Romans 2:28,29; 4:11). Later, by divine command, he guaranteed his covenant with Moses through bloody sacrifices (Hebrews 9:19-23). In the new covenant rite, the sacramental seal is the blood of God's own Son (Acts 20:28; Romans 3:25; 5:9; Ephesians 1:7). Putting a sacramental seal on us is a function common to Baptism and the Lord's Supper. But each sacrament has its distinct use in building God's church.

God's will confirmed

Jesus commanded Baptism uniquely as a *sacrament of initiation* into the New Testament church (Matthew 28:19). By Baptism we are enrolled in the church to become Jesus' followers. God the Father, as it were, signs our name on the certificate of church membership, God the Son seals it by his blood, and God the Holy Spirit delivers it by the gift of life-giving faith (Matthew 28:19). In a real and expressive way, Baptism is our first death and first resurrection (John 5:24; Revelation 20:5). By Baptism we die with Christ to sin and rise with Christ to new life (Romans 6:2-7). This makes a Christian's baptism a once-and-for-all-time occasion that need not be repeated, just as Christ's death and resurrection were unrepeatable, one-time happenings (Romans 6:8-10).

The Lord's Supper, by contrast, has been called the *sacrament of confirmation.* This sacrament constantly and repeatedly confirms the faith in Christ that Baptism works (1 Corinthians 11:26). In this respect, spiritual rebirth is similar to natural birth (John 3:5-8). We are born into this world only once yet we continually need to eat food to sustain life. Likewise, we are reborn only once but constantly need to partake of God's heavenly food to sustain new life in Christ. Why is this necessary?

As baptized Christians, we can stand before God as a holy people, completely reconciled and ready for service (1 Peter 2:9; Ephesians 2:10). Through faith in Jesus we are wholly righteous in his sight (Romans 3:22). We live in our baptism daily and richly. But we remain sinful and weak in our everyday walks through life. Our sinful flesh clings to us until our dying days and will not let go (Romans 7:14-20). Like a shaved beard, sin keeps on growing beneath the surface. We have not yet shuffled off our sinful flesh, not yet rid ourselves of daily trials and temptations.

In the wearisome daily struggle between our sinful flesh and God-given faith, we constantly need God's help and guidance. Sinful acts and attitudes make us wretched, and doubts plague our minds. But God is our refuge (Romans 7:14-25; Psalm 46:1). At such a time as this, God uses the holy gospel to give us certainty, hope, and comfort (Romans 8:31-39; Matthew 16:18,19; 18:18; John 20:21,22). At such a time as this, Christ strengthens our faith by placing before us a sacrament that visibly draws us to the cross. "Take, eat, and drink," he says in a literal simplicity that begs no question. "This is my body and my blood, given and shed for you for the forgiveness of sins."

Through Christ we take heart, repentantly and repeatedly calling on God and asking for mercy. In this quandary we find it foolish to ask, "What would Jesus do?" Thrown into God's arms, we ask by faith, "What has Jesus done for us?" (2 Corinthians 12:9; Hebrews 4:2). The answer lies in God's Word and promise. Through it, God first takes us to our baptism, where he put his name on us, adopted us through his Son, and gives us new life by his Spirit (Exodus 20:24; Isaiah 43:1; Matthew 28:19). And through his Word he then leads us to his Holy Supper, where he reassures us of his abiding presence. How is this done?

Baptism gives us the tangible new covenant sign of God's washing. The water of Baptism cleans us, not by washing dirt from the body. It cleanses us of filth and ungodliness that separate God and us, and it drowns our sinful selves by daily repentance (Titus 3:5-7). God once saved Noah from drowning in water by the very waters that upheld his ark (Genesis chapters 7,8). So water-baptism is like an ark-on-water that God prepared to save us from death. We sail on this ship through the troubled waters of life to our heavenly haven.

On the journey through life, God's Word and promise buoy us up. Not without reason we designate a church's assembly hall architecturally—and also significantly—as the *nave,* the Latin word for "ship." Baptism is our ship on the sea of life. It keeps us safe by pledging to give us a good conscience before God through our risen Savior and Lord (1 Peter 3:21). This ship remains seaworthy at all times, even if we jump ship by a godless life and unbelief. If by God's grace we return to faith, we take our place aboard again without needing to be rebaptized. God's grace and promises are constant amid the storms of life (2 Timothy 2:13).

By contrast, the Lord's Supper gives us the same tangible guarantee by ceremonial food, not water. As in Baptism, the visible elements in the Supper are not magical. The element of water itself does not save, but the Word of God that is in and with the water and the faith that trusts God's Word in the water do. Likewise, in his Supper God's food is not some magic potion that snaps us back to life, as happens in fairy tales.

The sacramental Supper is neither magical nor mythical. But in the highest sense it is a *mystery.* Eating Christ's meal returns us to the Garden of Eden. Its food takes us back to a life of pure delight (*Eden,* in Hebrew) with God. Just as the dedicated fruit on the tree of life in the Garden did, the Lord's Supper brings joy and delight. Not the fruit itself, but God's Word and promise make the food precious to eat (Genesis 2:8,9,15-17).

Then, as now, the sacramental meal remained God's mystery, especially designed to exercise our faith in God. But now we are receiving its delights *concealed* under earthly elements of bread and wine. The Holy Supper's chief function, therefore, is to be our new tree of life. The fruit of Jesus' death is the promise that partakers of his sacramental meal have life everlasting. The hungry eat of this tree of life and live righteous and whole before God for Jesus' sake. This good news strengthens and keeps us in the true faith unto life everlasting.

God's mystery unveiled

The divine mystery reveals God's eternal love in a way vastly different from mysteries of the created universe (Job 38:4-41). The critical difference between life's unsolved mysteries and God's divine mystery of salvation is found in the person of Jesus the Christ. Human wisdom scientifically probes mysteries of the earth yet unknown. God, by contrast, does the opposite. He wisely makes the mystery of his saving love *known* in the cross (1 Corinthians 1:22-25). The cross makes God's redemptive mystery more than a mere sign of something sacred and hidden to our eyes. On Good Friday, God *openly revealed* his sacred secret to mankind in the person of Jesus Christ.

Paul uses carefully measured and emphatic words to explain the mystery of the cross: "We speak of God's *secret* wisdom, a wisdom that has been *hidden* and that God destined for our glory before time began. None of the rulers of this age understood it, for if they had, they would not have crucified the Lord of glory. However, as it is written: 'No eye has seen, no ear has heard, no mind has conceived what God has prepared for those who love him'—but God has *revealed* it to us by his Spirit" (1 Corinthians 2:7-10). What does Paul mean when he says that God revealed a secret?

The answer lies in the way God *reveals* himself so we can come *into his presence* (Numbers 6:24-26). His divine revelation to mortals touches on the secret of his glory and majesty. In his superior wisdom, God chose to reveal himself in a way unknown to the world, in a manner beyond human experience, in a *mystery* that demands faith (1 Corinthians 2:10-16). In God's own way, faith is not a leap in the dark but a divine gift that latches on to an object (Hebrews 11:1). That object is Christ—revealed in his Word, hidden in his Supper.

In human experience, something revealed is no longer concealed. A butterfly, as we have previously observed, unveils its beauty to show a stunning array of colors by *coming out of* its hiding in a chrysalis. But when God reveals his life-changing glory, he reverses the order. God reveals himself by *going into hiding*. God, as he is, is already hidden from us in his majesty. We only sense him from observing nature and the majestic universe that surrounds us (Romans 1:19,20).

But now the hidden God hides himself again (Isaiah 45:15). In a twofold hiding, God conceals himself once more—this time in what we can see and observe with human eyes. God *goes into* hiding by concealing himself in mortal flesh (Matthew 17:1-8). Our eyes see Jesus on the cross, a human being as we are. We can observe a human dying an agonizing death. In his crucifixion there is no dazzling display of beauty to attract us, no butterfly effect (Isaiah 53:2-12). Just the opposite!

Yet the one dying is our God. He has cloaked his majesty as God. He dies a convict, bearing the stripes of the guilty in the manner we humans regard legal justice. He reveals his glory in shame and his strength in the weakness of death-by-crucifixion. The cross is not glorious. It is our electric chair, an instrument of torture, and it produces an excruciating death (Luke 23:32-37). Only by faith can we *see* what is happening beneath the cloak of Jesus' humanity. The robe of guilt Jesus wears is ours. Only by faith can we understand the joyous exchange that is taking place on that day of infamy in Jerusalem. It is a moment to remember for a most intimate reason.

God's pledge of love
In the paradox of life, the King of kings and the Lord of lords comes down from heaven and picks us up off the streets of this world—poor little prostitutes that we are. He wills to marry us who have been lusting after other gods and have nothing to offer him but our self-centered sinful lifestyles (Hosea 1:2; Exodus 20:3). And he puts on our fingers the wedding ring of faith. The heavenly Bridegroom takes our sins as his dowry (Isaiah 53:6). In exchange he gives his unworthy brides all that is his—life with God, peace and joy, and salvation. He forgives our waywardness, puts aside his anger, and freely declares his love for us once more (Hosea 14:1-4; Song of Songs 4:1; Isaiah 44:2).

Now in the glorious union of bride and groom, he becomes our sin and we are his righteousness. The crucified covers his bride's filthiness with a pure white wedding dress of his making (Revelation 6:11; Isaiah 61:10). The Bridegroom's death removes sin's sting, and his resurrection to life tears down death's barrier for a simple reason.

That powerful duo—sin and death—has kept us from enjoying life (1 Corinthians 15:54-57). Christ's righteousness replaces the holiness long lost in paradise. Christ Jesus makes his bride God's own prize possession once again (Isaiah 53:6-10; Genesis 1:27,28; Revelation 19:6-9). For the Crucified is our God. He is God and man in an indivisible and eternal union. Faith alone grasps the mystery of God's work on earth and receives its benefits. How is this done?

The holy meal is God's way of pledging his love for us freely and openly. But the Communion meal remains a mystery—God's mystery. *How* Jesus' body and blood can be sacramentally united with fruits of the field defies human explanation. *How* Jesus himself becomes one with us remains a union as mystical as man and wife becoming one flesh (Genesis 2:24; 1 Corinthians 10:16,17). Yet the Lord of the feast wants us to know this regarding his pledge of love: Bread and wine are much more than a sign of Jesus' presence. The Lord gives us his body, just as, in an earthly parallel, a bridegroom gives his body to his bride. Jesus is there for us in the manner that he says, "This is my body . . . my blood." The little word *this* holds the key to the mystery.

Through the little word *this*, God's Spirit takes us behind the veil to see what is really happening (John 15:26; 1 Corinthians 2:10-16). He leads us to comprehend the mystery of God's love. He unveils what is hidden to our eyes as we open our mouths to receive. There—hidden under the form of bread and wine—are the true body and blood of the risen Lord (1 John 1:7). The Lamb's high feast is a powerful pledge and gracious seal of God's will to the undeserving. "This do" is God's sacred "I do," as if spoken in a marriage vow.

Care in the Supper's use

As the years passed by, the Christian church began more and more to investigate the sacramental mystery and its use in the church. Under pressure of people's questioning, clerics and scholars frequently discussed the nature of Jesus' presence at his Supper. Arguments became heated, highly sophisticated, and philosophical. Answers were played out on the checkerboard of reason. Many insights contained kernels of truth. But the debate often resulted in one-sided attempts to solve the unsolvable mystery of Christ's presence. And, sadly, the argumentation eventually divided Christ's church and hindered the Supper's service to the church (John 17:17-21; 1 Corinthians 1:10-13).

The debate focused particularly on Jesus' simple phrase: "This is my body." Scholars dissected, explained, and interpreted each of Jesus' words. They brought grammar, logic, and history to bear on the problems of interpretation. Yet the deeper church leaders attempted to probe the mystery, the more confused the issues—and the people—became.

Some, then as now, limit the meaning of body/blood. They rightly highlight the Sacrament's first use, an *outward sign* of God's presence on earth. At the same time, they virtually deny Jesus' bodily presence in the Supper and its service as a seal of forgiveness. Use of bread and wine then comes to signify only Jesus' *spiritual* presence, an external mark of Christ's absent body. As a result, the Supper becomes a mere memorial meal to Jesus, who is present in his Supper spiritually but is not there bodily.

Others, then as now, rightly stress the Sacrament's second use. They consider Jesus' presence to be primarily a *seal and guarantee* of God's forgiving love for us. And they vigorously maintain that Jesus is present in body for good reason. At the meal he seals his grace to us personally and

unites us to himself into one body (1 Corinthians
10:16,17). When Jesus says, "This is my body," he means
he is present *bodily*. All who partake of the blessed bread
and drink from the consecrated cup receive what Jesus
promises in his Word. After all, the sacramental meal is
worked by God. He prepares the Holy Supper as a host
readies a meal for guests. Human hands and voice mask
what God works through his Word (Isaiah 55:11).

This explanation does two things. It avoids the claim
that Jesus is present only in my faith, making the festive
meal to be a mere spiritual eating on my part. Even more
directly, it emphatically acknowledges the bodily presence
of the Lord Jesus Christ in the Sacrament.

Obscuring the mystery: Real presence by change in substance

Later developments clouded valid Christian expressions
and concerns. In the Western church, centered in Rome,
authorities gave finely structured, sophisticated answers to
Jesus' bodily presence at the Lord's Supper. They pointed
out how Jesus' sacrifice on Good Friday differs uniquely
from the church's act at an earthly altar. Consequently,
clerics separated Christ's one-time bodily sacrifice on Calvary from Christ's ongoing appearance in the Lord's Supper. The manner of sacrifice is said to differ significantly.
On the cross, they observed, Christ was sacrificed in his
body *as it was then*. But in the Supper he sacrifices in his
body *as it is now*. What does this distinction mean?

At the crucifixion, it is said, Jesus had a *physical* body as
the instrument of sacrifice. His sacrifice on Calvary was
bloody. But now Jesus has a *spiritual* body through which
he acts and sacrifices. This body is the church, of which
he is the head (Ephesians 1:22). As Christ's *body now*, the
church sacrifices at the altar—but with this difference.

Now the sacrifice at the church's altar is unbloody. No physical bloodshed takes place. The church simply continues Christ's one-time sacrifice by repeated action. The sacramental meal offers an unbloody repetition of the bloody sacrifice of Christ on Calvary.

In this way clerics of the Western church sought to clarify two nagging questions: How is Jesus bodily present in the meal? and how does the mystery of Jesus' bodily presence take place? In answer they focused on the priestly action at the altar just as it happened under Israel's priestly covenant in the Old Testament. Now the church brings an offering of bread and wine to the altar and through its clergy offers these fruits of the field in thanksgiving to God. At the priestly consecration, bread and wine are set aside and are converted into Christ's body and blood. The bread—still apparently bread—acts to host Christ's body. Eyes cannot observe a change, and those who eat still taste bread. But the changeover from bread to Christ's body and from wine to Christ's blood takes place supernaturally in the heavenly realm of a two-storied universe.

Behind this extensive explanation a number of things are clear. There is a shift in the Supper's focus from Christ's body (in the Sacrament) to the body of Christ (the church), from Christ's work on the cross to the church's priestly action at the altar. As the body of Christ, the church *continues the work* at the altar that Christ once did on the cross. As Christ's body now, the church performs a *propitiatory sacrifice* to satisfy, sweeten, and appease God's anger over sin. In so doing, offerings of bread and wine are said to lose their *natural* substance. What was bread is now Christ's body and wine is his blood. This substance change (transubstantiation) is said to take place according to a special understanding of what is real.

If the explanation puzzles us, we need to ask the question, What is real? This question lies at the heart of the debate over the *real presence* of Christ in the Lord's Supper. It is the question that moves the apostle Paul to write, "The *reality* . . . is found in Christ" (Colossians 2:17).

Understanding what is real

Questions concerning reality are common to our everyday life to this day. They come up each time we blurt out, "Get real!" or "Really?" In pursuing this basic question of life, one school in the Western church contends that our world, as we experience it, is not really real. This school believes we live on earth as if in shadowlands. Our world only *appears* real, just as shadows on a wall look real but they only reflect objects. Things on earth—including such things as bread/wine and body/blood—are said to be like shadows. Earthly elements are then just shadow phenomena. They only reflect God, the Maker of the earth. Everything on earth gains its reality from God, just as shadows reflect what is behind them.

This way of reasoning influenced Western clerics in their explanation of the mystery of the Lord's Supper. So, for bread to become Christ's body, the changeover obviously does not take place in the shadowlands here below. In our world, bread (incidentally) remains bread. We see it; we taste it. The real change from bread to Christ's body is said to take place with God above, beyond our natural world, in the upper story of a two-storied universe. By God's design, what looks like bread in reality becomes Jesus' body.

How is this possible? The realist school says God can do such things because only he is real. God once identified himself to Moses by the personal name "I AM" (Exodus

3:11-14). This majestic name of God is the name of the all-powerful being. Reverently, the Israelites referred to God as "HE IS," in the way underlings refer to their king. Spoken in Hebrew, they called him *Yahweh*, the name that in English is translated "LORD" (Exodus 34:6,7). This almighty "LORD" not only possesses power but energetically uses his power to help us in our need.

At the Supper, therefore, the explanation ends. God exercises his power from above by repeatedly changing bread into Jesus' body and wine into Jesus' blood. And significantly he brings about this change by acting through his body *as it is now*, that is, through the church. The church is sacrificing. Through its clergy the *church* forms the sacrificial bridge to bring about Christ's real presence in the Lord's Supper.

Obscuring the mystery: Real presence spiritually

Opponents of the realist school say no to this manner of thinking. Such an approach to Jesus' Supper, they argue, is too sophisticated. It weaves in and out of God's truth. It explains the mystery but leaves little, if any, room for a person's faith. The Supper is turned into a formal churchly act that becomes a sacrifice and work *on our part*. God formerly despised the Israelites' sacrifices when carried out *merely by doing the work* perfunctorily or by mere performance (Latin: *ex opere operato*) (Amos 5:21-25).

It appears that the Holy Sacrament has become an act done meritoriously by corporate church rather than graciously by God's Word and promise. Above all, the question still remains: Why is God's sacrifice *repeatedly redone* when it was finished and perfected once for all in the past (Hebrews 7:26,27)? In trying to be objective, the realist school has gone too far. It makes Jesus' body into a thing

so that people bow to it as to an idol, carry it about in pro-
cessions, and store it in a tabernacle. Christ's one-time
atoning sacrifice has gotten lost in churchly use and power.
Critics trace the problem simply to a faulty view of reality,
and they seek to explain the real presence of Christ in a
totally different way.

According to the scientific school, the opposite actually
is true. Reality does not lie *beyond* the boundaries of our
natural world but *in nature* itself. The earth is real. This
world is real. Things are real. We name, identify, and scientifically classify things in our universe. Like Adam of
old, we give names to animals, birds, sea creatures, flowers
and fauna, and planets and stars that we can see, touch,
and enjoy (Genesis 2:19,20). We actually live in the *real
world,* not in shadowlands. Certainly, God is real also. He
is the great "I AM." But to know him is to *believe* in him
(Hebrews 11:1-3). In the pictured two-storied universe,
the gap between the real world below and the divine world
above is bridged by a person's faith.

How then, according to this school, do we receive
Christ's body in his Supper? Jesus is said to have answered
the question at the last Passover in the simplest way possible. He asked us to eat the new Supper *in remembrance* of
him. As we hear Jesus' words, "This is my body," and eat
plain bread, our faith reaches up into heaven above and
there, not in the bread, we receive our Lord. In other
words, ours is a *faith eating.* Bread does not really change. It
remains nothing but a plain piece of bread and acts merely
as a *noteworthy sign* to mark Jesus' presence. In reality,
therefore, we receive Jesus' body *spiritually by faith, not
orally* in our mouths. Faith solves the mystery of the Holy
Supper by leaving Jesus' body in heaven above where he
lives and rules.

To think otherwise is said to beg a basic question: If Jesus ascended to heaven and is now seated at God's right hand, must he not be located in heaven? How can his body be present in two places at one time? A body has limits and limitations. Bodies occupy space—and are confined to it. That is a scientific truth. A body cannot be in heaven above and on earth below at one and the same time. It is unnatural and illogical even to imagine that Jesus is really present in bodily form everywhere all over the world. The Bible says so. The biblical record is said to affirm that Jesus is *locally* seated at the right hand of the almighty God (Matthew 26:64; Mark 16:19; Luke 20:42; Psalm 110:1).

If that is the case, then what happens at his Supper? On hearing his command to eat, "This do," we are merely to obey it. We eat bread in blessed memory of Jesus' death because our Savior asked us to do this. And as we eat, our faith reaches into heaven above and there, not in bread, we partake of Jesus' body spiritually. Certainly we can talk about Jesus being *really present*. But by that we mean he is only *spiritually present*. Bread and wine are nothing but graphic earthly *representations* of Christ's absent body and blood. Seeing bread and wine and hearing his words vividly bring to mind Christ's awesome work for us on the cross. But the food we eat at the Lord's Table is *really* only an *outward mark* of an inward spiritual happening—nothing more, nothing less.

Real presence sacramentally

One-sided explanations of the Lord's presence in his Supper attempt to answer people's questions sincerely. They captivate people's minds with complex views of reality, or they turn people off to religion because of their sophistry. Listening, we may be torn both ways or be overwhelmed by them as were early Christians in Colosse (Colossians 2:8-20). In frustration, many people throw up their hands and accept explanations merely on churchly authority. They frankly admit, "I believe whatever the church believes."

In the process, Jesus' words fall short of God's intended mark. Interpretations that aim at the heart must never lose sight of the *whole* picture of God's words of love nor bypass God's views of his presence (Matthew 28:20). Errant ways, God warns, most often veer from the truth by becoming partial truths (Deuteronomy 5:32). And half-truths obscure truths one-sidedly. We are brought back to God's truth only when we return to Eden, listen to God's Word, and by God's grace walk the middle way of faith.

Already in Eden the arch-deceiver, armed with God's Word, sought to lead people astray by half-truths. He cleverly challenged God's words with respect to dedicated food. A seemingly innocent question, "Did God *really* say, 'You must not eat . . . ?'" casted doubt on God's Word. It cunningly obscured and misrepresented God's intentions (Genesis 3:1-4). Self-generated interpretations always fail to take God at his Word and, therefore, fail to let God's Word be its own interpreter. Like philosophers, such interpreters peel God's mysteries apart. They separate our world from God's world with subtle distinctions. So the mystery of God's work remains hidden and obscure to us (Isaiah 45:15). As soon as we try to penetrate God's ways by our own thinking or doing, God's work on earth stays veiled and unknown (1 Corinthians 2:10-13; Acts 17:23).

When all is said and done, we cannot comprehend God, the great "I AM." We have no power to put God in a box, much less to come into his gracious presence on our own (1 Corinthians 1:26-31). God is formless and infinite in his being and knows no human bounds. *How* God then can be present under the form of bread will always boggle earth-bound minds. Asking how in this case is like investigating the mystery of Christ's incarnation. Faced with an unsolvable question—how could God be confined in the virgin Mary's womb?—we fail in answering. We are at a loss to explain naturally or philosophically how the infinite God could take on finite flesh.

But God's Spirit makes the answer clear and simple for all who trust him and rely on his Word. God solves the mystery of his presence by taking the initiative. In love he sent his Son into our world. Jesus the Messiah came from the Father's side (John 3:16; 1:18). Faith always has an *object* to cling to. Jesus is the object of our faith. In him we are able to see the Creator of all things *visibly* and to hear his Word *audibly* (Mark 9:7). The Son of Man acts on our streets and speaks to us about God's kingdom (John 1:1-3,14; 10:30; Acts 1:3).

Mystery of mysteries, God himself entered his creation, took on human form, and personally united himself with us in a miraculous way (John 15:1-8). In his person, Jesus—Son of God and Son of Man—united heaven above and the earth below. The infinite God appeared on our finite earth, the real God in our real world. Jesus is God's answer to all questions about God's love and his gracious presence (John 14:8-14). He alone bridges the gap between earth and heaven. He alone reopens the door to life that once slammed shut when Satan questioned God's Word and we believed him rather than God (John 1:51; Genesis 2:9; 3:22). We can only worship and adore the child on Mary's lap (Luke 2:33-35).

Now no further speculation is needed—no more vain debates about reality and shadow phenomena, no two-

storied universe, no gaps for sinful people to bridge. Jesus
embodies all that is real in heaven above and earth below
(Colossians 2:17). To the question of the ages—why did
God become man?—God gives a simple but dynamic
answer (John 3:16; Romans 1:16). God's one and only
begotten Son came to earth to remove sin's veil that blinds
us to God's presence (John 1:18). God entered his created
world to redeem us from captivity to evil (Ephesians 1:7;
Matthew 6:13; Psalm 68:18). God died so we should never
die again or live apart from the source of life forever
(Hebrews 10:19-22). Jesus is God's Word *to* us and *for* us.
He is the *Word in the Word* on record in the Holy Writings
and has spoken to us in the holy gospel (John 1:1,16-18).

The mystery of God's real presence in his Holy Supper,
therefore, lies in Christ. No other bridge builder is needed.
The One who united heaven above and earth below in his
person gives us the joy of eating at the Lamb's high feast
(Colossians 2:9,10). To know Jesus is to know God (John
10:30; 14:11). To know God is to love him (1 John 4:19).
To love God is to come into his presence without fear
(Psalm 24:3-5). To stand before God is to sing loudly the
church's bridal song on earth, a song echoed in heaven:
"Salvation belongs to our God, who sits on the throne,
and to the Lamb" (Revelation 7:10). "Holy is his name"
(Luke 1:49; Isaiah 6:3). In the Lord's Supper, the Bridegroom brings his bride into the presence of God himself
with thanks (Revelation 21:9,10; 5:13,14). At the Lamb's
high feast we stand in joy beside him.

Presence of Christ on earth

Jesus our Redeemer, therefore, never loses his humanness, neither in heaven above nor on earth below. Only to
our detriment do we divide Christ in two and have a

divine Christ and a human Christ. Only to our confusion do we physically separate the world of nature from the spiritual world as philosophers do. Jesus unites heaven and earth in his person for a simple and singular reason. He claims supremacy over all things in heaven and earth and reconciles the two before God (Colossians 1:18). This is the holy gospel in a nutshell.

For our sake Paul puts God's glorious mission/vision statement into simple and uplifting words. He proclaims the whole counsel of God and unfolds the mystery of God at work on earth in a most personal and universal way (Colossians 1:15-23). God's mission statement focuses on Christ. He is the head of all things. Anyone who usurps Christ's role as the church's head by divine right challenges Jesus' supremacy as the world's Redeemer and reconciler (2 Thessalonians 2:3,4). The apostle takes pains to explain the importance of Christ's work to all who rely on hollow and deceptive talk rather than on God's Word. And he purposefully puts the mystery of Christ's work into historical perspective (Colossians 2:8).

In an unparalleled description of God's grand vision for the world, Paul reveals how Jesus unites heaven and earth in his person, first of all, for God's *good* purposes. He puts special emphasis on the *things* of creation as a way to describe our world. In this way we come to fear, love, and trust in God above all *things*, the Creator above his creation:

> By [Christ] all *things* were created: *things* in heaven and on earth, visible and invisible, whether thrones or powers or rulers or authorities; *all things* were created by him and for him. He is before *all things*, and in him *all things* hold together. (Colossians 1:16,17)

But God's grand view continues uniquely. God's creation simultaneously intersects with God's church. Jesus is also head of the church. And he unites the church in his person, calling the church his body—to accomplish God's *gracious* ends. In this way God's good will and his gracious will unite to show his love for us. At the center of all is Jesus' blood, shed on the cross:

> And he [Christ] is *the head of the body, the church;* he is the beginning and the firstborn from among the dead, so that in everything he might have the *supremacy.* For God was pleased to have all his fullness dwell in him, and through him *to reconcile to himself all things,* whether *things on earth or things in heaven,* by making peace through his blood, shed on the cross. (Colossians 1:18-20)

The truth is out! In Christ Jesus questions regarding what is real are answered with crystal clarity. Jesus reveals the real God in our real world (John 14:9-11). As the "image of the invisible God," Mary's child is the firstborn over all creation (Colossians 1:15). He is one person, not two. His humanness shares in the work of his divine self. If the divine Christ by his very nature as God is everywhere, he is always there as the bloodstained crucified.

God's own blood redeems us, as the apostle points out with measured words (Acts 20:28). God wants us to know that he has blood—but only because God became man, only because God's Son took on a servant's form, only because he is really as human as we are, only because blood is the seat of life in God's sight, as each Passover lamb demonstrated (Leviticus 17:11; Romans 3:25). To this truth all Scriptures bear witness, from the original promise heard by Adam and Abraham to the Passover and the holy meal (Acts 20:28).

Presence of Christ in the Supper

God's mystery continues through time into eternity. The crucified who walked the earth also rose, left the earth, and ascended to heaven (John 7:33,34). The exalted Son did not jettison his humanity when he entered heaven (Revelation 5:6-10). The Lamb that was sacrificed still lives as the Lamb that was slain for us. Exalted on high, Jesus lives and rules at God's right hand in a position of judgment (Psalm 110:1; Matthew 26:64; Hebrews 1:3). The ascended Lord carries out his Father's rule in both places—heaven and earth (1 Corinthians 15:25-28). He promised he would never leave us on earth without his presence (Matthew 28:20; John 14:18). And he personally comes to us earthlings as he wills (1 Corinthians 15:25-27)—his presence *hidden* both in providential care and in merciful forgiveness.

Wherever the Lord's Table is set, therefore, our Lord is there. His human nature fully shares the work of his divine being (Psalm 139:7-10; Jeremiah 23:24). His meal is ours to enjoy. The message is God's to give: "This is my body . . . for many for the forgiveness of sins." It is the message of God's love for us in Christ, proclaimed openly to the world and sealed personally by his presence in his Supper under his ordained form of bread/wine. There, by invitation, he intimately draws us to his side (John 1:18). There, in his presence, God unfolds the sacred secret revealed on the cross—the mystery of how Jesus reconciles God and the world. How is this done?

Real presence of Christ crucified

For God to be God—holy, true, and just—he does not overlook our sins. We cannot be reconciled just because "we're sorry" for mocking God by self-centered lives and unholy living. Reconciliation does not come simply because God changes his mind or we change our attitudes (Malachi 3:6; James 1:16-18; Ephesians 2:3-5). The chasm between God and us is too deep for reconciliation to be a mere kiss-and-make-up act as happens between people (Psalm 130).

Reconciliation between God and humankind comes solely through a third party who, as is the case, intervenes and takes up our cause. Reconciliation remains an act of God's love, an act of the One who sent his Son to be our go-between (Job 19:25). God's Son acts to undo the fateful divorce that separates God above and sinners below. We are reconciled to God only through Christ. Only in Christ's redeeming death are we forgiven and do we begin life with a fresh attitude toward God, toward the world, toward our neighbors, and all creation (2 Corinthians 5:19).

The One who unites heaven with earth has acted with a clearly focused mission. God's mission statement in summary is this: God "has reconciled you by Christ's *physical body* through death to present you holy in his sight, without blemish and free from accusation—if you continue in your faith, established and firm, not moved from the hope held out in the gospel" (Colossians 1:22,23). The Sacrament of the Altar firms up our faith and pledges God's faithfulness to us. It brings Christ to us by the Lord's special commitment. "Take and eat," Jesus says as he extends to us the bread set aside in thanksgiving for God's loving-kindness. "This is my body . . . for many for the forgiveness of sins."

In the light of God's action, to imagine that the Lord in heaven extends his body *physically* everywhere on earth is clearly a misnomer. When we eat the Lord's Supper, Christians are not cannibals, as some mistakenly charge.

Our risen Lord is present bodily because he is one person with a human nature and a divine nature that are insepa-rably united. After Jesus rose from death, he did not sud-denly shed his body like the butterfly jettisons its cocoon. His glorified body now shares fully and continually in his majesty as God. Since God by his very nature is every-where, the Lamb that was slain for us is everywhere. Wherever the ascended Lord wills to be, he breaks the limits of time and space. If God wills to be present bodily under the form of bread, so be it. Jesus' resurrected body is there for us.

How did Jesus communicate this? Jesus expressed his holy will for us in his final supper before death. At the Passover celebration, he anticipated his continuing pres-ence after death. At this high festival he gave God thanks, extended a cup, and offered his followers a new covenant guaranteed by Word and deed: "This is my blood of the covenant," he said, "which is poured out for many for the forgiveness of sins" (Matthew 26:28). There at the table the Lord of all creation willed to be present with us from that time onward, hidden under the elements of bread and wine. And he now makes his will known in the food we see and the meal we eat. "This is my body . . . my blood," he says in direct words of promise. And his Word is truth (John 8:31,32; 14:6).

In the long run, the lesson to Christ's people is simply this: For the sake of teaching we can *distinguish* our Sav-ior's divine nature from his human nature as the Scriptures do (Mark 1:11; 2:28). Jesus is Son of God and Son of Man. But we dare not *divide* Christ in two and make two Christs, one divine and one human, as if the two merely had names in common. Such a scientific approach undoes the mystery of God's love in Christ.

Equally harmful to the work of Christ is to *mix* Jesus' divine and human natures into one without distinguishing the one from the other. Early Christians expressly recognized that human beings have limited characteristics but that God has unlimited. If we mix the two together in Jesus, then Jesus' unlimited divinity would overpower the limitations of his humanity. Then Jesus' earthly life would mean that God was merely playacting, and Jesus' death for our sins would become an act of a superman—with negative consequences for faith and life.

Then, as a result, Jesus' passion would be no longer the work of a fully human person who carried our weaknesses yet was without sin. Jesus' cross would be no longer the real sacrificial act of the Suffering Servant. As a consequence, our redemption would be at stake. All this despite the prophet's clear testimony to the Christ: "He was despised and rejected by men, a man of sorrows, and familiar with suffering. . . . Surely he took up our infirmities and carried our sorrows, yet we considered him stricken by God, smitten by him, and afflicted. But he was pierced for our transgressions . . . and by his wounds we are healed" (Isaiah 53:3-5).

When all is said and done, it is Jesus' *human flesh* that is the stumbling block to faith. That *this human being* is God causes faith to shipwreck (John 6:57,58,66). That *this man* is God was blatant blasphemy to Jewish authorities and still remains intolerable to our natural senses and human sensitivities (Luke 22:66-71). To look at this human being in mockery on the cross, an object of shame and weakness, and to say, "This person is our God," is an insurmountable problem for one basic reason: We are all by nature anti-Christ (1 John 4:1-3). Only the person who "acknowledges that Jesus Christ has come *in the flesh* is from God" (1 John 4:2).

How then does Jesus want us to understand his presence in heaven as on earth? The church of the apostles answered in a historic hymn to Christ. This Christ-hymn shows how God took action to shape us to his way of thinking (Philippians 2:5). The song traces Christ's work in two stages. The first stage highlights Christ's life on earth. The second stage celebrates Christ's rule in heaven. The first stanza sings of Christ, our Redeemer, in humiliation. The second hails Jesus, our Lord, in exaltation. This glorious litany traces the span of Christ's mission from eternity to eternity (Philippians 2:6-11). Even without a melody to follow, we can sing the Lord Jesus' biography in our hearts with a slow and careful reading of the descriptive words:

Who, being in very nature God,
did not consider equality with God something to be grasped,
but made himself nothing,
taking the very nature of a servant,
being made in human likeness.
And being found in appearance as a man,
he *humbled himself*
and became obedient to death—even death on a cross!

Therefore God *exalted* him to the highest place
and gave him the name that is above every name,
that at the name of Jesus [his human name] every knee should bow,
in heaven and on earth and under the earth,
and every tongue confess that
Jesus Christ is Lord,
to the glory of God the Father.

So unveils the mystery of our Savior and Lord, Jesus the Christ. On earth the Lord divested himself of his divinity, hid his divinity under a servant's form, and assumed our flesh and blood for a reason. He identified with our plight, was truly tempted as we are, and really died as we do. The occasional outbursts of his divine power on earth in miracles and epiphanies were not meant to astound. They showed his authority over life, indicated that he cares, and proved his Savior-love for all mankind (Mark 2:10-12). We sing the mystery of God's love although we cannot understand it. We believe in Christ, but we cannot comprehend him.

Christ's legacy of love

After his victory in the battle for life, the Lamb of God willed to leave his legacy of love under the form of a holy sacrament. He gave no lengthy explanations on how his body and blood serves the church. He only gave us a personal answer. He offered us a communion of bread and wine and his body and blood to unite us with himself, the head with the body, and to strengthen our faith in him (1 Corinthians 10:15,16). The church, therefore, uses the Lord's Supper rightly for the purpose of confirming and strengthening faith.

Jesus' life on earth is testimony enough to the truth of his heavenly gift. Because Jesus is who he is, we go boldly to celebrate the Lamb's high feast. At the table we receive Christ exactly as our host promises: "Take and eat. This is my body . . . for many for the forgiveness of sins." Bread visible to the eye and real to the taste is a mark of Christ's church for all to see. More than a sign, Christ's body seals our forgiveness before God.

No matter when or where we come into God's presence and receive grace in his Supper, we can leave at peace, guilt free, forgiven, and free to serve. We live each moment of our earthly lives in intimate union with the One who frees us, as an unworthy bride rejoices in her loving Bridegroom (Ephesians 5:22-32). In thanksgiving we are now at liberty to serve God with songs of worship and praise. Forgiven, we stand ready to give ourselves to others with a whole new attitude on life (Galatians 5:1-6). Such faith activates us (James 2:14-17). Our helpful deeds of love and charity in church and society bring God praise and honor for his marvelous gift (Ephesians 2:8-10; Matthew 5:16).

5

Celebrating the Lord's Supper

The Lord Jesus purposefully arranged a festive meal that would extend past time and space into eternity. Each time we eat the Lamb's high feast, he focuses our lives on God's grand goal: "to bring all things in heaven and on earth together under one head, even Christ" (Ephesians 1:10). The oneness that Christians have through time and eternity is found in Christ alone and in his Supper. Eating at the Lord's Table here is a foretaste of dining at the heavenly table there, where saints are already gathered in God's presence (Luke 22:29,30; Isaiah 25:6; Hebrews 12:1,2). Returning to Eden now to eat of the tree of life merely precedes entering paradise to celebrate life with God eternally (Revelation 7:15-17; 2:7; 22:14,19).

In anticipation of future glory, Christ presented himself at a festive table spread with bread and wine. For such a time as this, Christ comes to us under the cover of this earthly food. He intentionally condescended to come in a lowly manner—the hidden God in hidden form. He anticipates the day when the veil will drop from his radiant face and sin's blindfold will no longer block our view of him (Isaiah 25:7,8; Matthew 17:2; 1 Corinthians 13:12). On that day all creation will face the Lord as a gracious King and righteous judge (Philippians 2:9-11; Matthew 25:31-46). One of the blessings that awaits God's people, according to Revelation, comes in banquet terms: "Blessed are those who are invited to the wedding supper of the Lamb!" (Revelation 19:9).

God's gracious summons

As a measure of God's mission, Jesus extended a worldwide invitation to every tribe and people. He commissioned and still commissions his followers to spread the Word of Life to all nations, to assemble believers by Baptism, and to nurture faith by instruction (Matthew 28:16-20; John 3:16). The invitation simply reads, "Come to me, all you who are weary and burdened, and I will give you rest" (Matthew 11:28; Exodus 33:14; Deuteronomy 12:10). Christ's rest is unique on earth. To live with Christ means to die to sin and set aside our old way of life. He promises a way of life freed from sin, at peace in spirit, and at one with God. This promise is meant for all whom the Lord God calls (Acts 2:36-41).

With understandable caution, therefore, Jesus warns people not to take his invitation lightly (Mark 2:15-17). His outreach to us is a matter of grace, pure and simple (Matthew 22:1-14). To reject Jesus as the living bread from heaven that sustains life is to rebuff God himself (John 6:25-66; 8:42-47). Yet, in spite of the warning, self-satisfied people consider Jesus' promise to be foolishness and his Word nonsense (1 Corinthians 1:20-25). Non-takers continue to wallow in a wayward way of life like pigs or parade their own goodness before God like peacocks (Galatians 5:19-21; Luke 18:9-14). To their eventual sorrow, both bypass the Savior's open invitation to come to him for rest (Luke 19:7-9; 1 Corinthians 11:27-29).

A special invitation

Warnings against rejecting God's gracious call become doubly earnest for those who celebrate the Lord's Supper (Hebrews 3:7-11). At the Lamb's high feast, our Lord makes his invitation specific and special on purpose. The table is set for believers only. The Lord reserves this divine mystery for the faithful and closes the Communion table to the impious and unbelievers for good reason. At his Supper Jesus offers food, not to vitalize body strength but to energize and strengthen *faith*. He sets the banquet table for those who openly or privately confess their sin and come to him in need of God's favor and forgiveness (Luke 5:5-8; Isaiah 6:1-5). That is precisely why Jesus summons beggars to a meal fit for a king and regards their lowliness and unworthiness.

Many Christians might misunderstand the invitation to the Lord's Supper on this account. We hesitate to come to the Lord's Table because we feel we are not good enough to attend. In self-centered confusion, we measure our worthiness by other "good" Christians. But Jesus does not measure qualifications for attendance by character or comparison. On that basis no one would be good enough to come into the presence of the holy God, much less dine with him (Psalm 24:4). God's prophet strikingly reminds us that "all of us have become like one who is unclean, and all our righteous acts are like filthy rags" (Isaiah 64:6).

To the question of who then is worthy to come to the Lord's Supper, the answer is simple. Christ alone is our worthiness (Revelation 5:12-14). Christ alone makes the downcast fit to stand in God's presence. He alone fills empty hearts with his abiding presence and sends the self-satisfied away empty (Luke 1:46-55). We need not posture for position in the banquet line. Jesus does not require that we must merit his food. Like victims of natural disasters, victims of evil come to God just as they are, without concern about self-image or self-worth. At the table we are sinners in the hands of a gracious God who knows our needs. What does this mean?

Need for God's rest is evident from our daily misconduct (Hebrews 3:12-15). Obvious wrongs are not the least of miseries that bother consciences and affect our daily walks through life (Galatians 5:19-21). Disobedience, murder, sexual immorality, theft, lying, deceiving, disregard for others, hating, cheating, and coveting—who can measure them all!—are acts dealt with in civil courts of law as well as in the court of God's justice (the Law—Exodus 20:12-17). Human freedom and human rights do not give us license to live as we please or to act in disregard for God and our neighbors. Such gross and immoral ways are manifest in the daily news media. Persisting in a libertine lifestyle excludes us from life with God and a seat at the festival table.

But subtle sins also cry to high heaven. Not merely what we do but what we fail to do for others condemns us before God (Matthew 25:41-46). Human judges convict persons because they are lawbreakers, not because they are sinners.

But God is a divine judge who convicts people of sin. In God's court the royal law of love demands a perfection we lack by nature (James 1:19–2:17). For this reason moralists and legalists constantly dance on eggs in vain attempts to keep the law of love to perfection (James 2:10-12; Romans 7:23-25; Galatians 2:17-21).

The root of the problem is that our sinful selves lack true fear and faith in God from birth (Psalm 51:5; Romans 3:10-18). Therefore, topping the list of sinful deeds and attitudes is our disregard for God himself (Exodus 20:3-11). God's case against us is rock solid, and we deserve life apart from him forever in everlasting punishment (Matthew 25:41-46). As one experienced Christian openly confessed to God, "You have created us for yourself, and our hearts cannot be quieted until they find rest in you!"

Out of the depths of despair, therefore, we look to God for aid (Psalm 130:1-4; 51:1-4; Romans 7:22-25; 8:26,27). God hears our cries and confirms his promise of a new life in Christ (Genesis 1:27,28; 2:7; 3:15). God's Spirit renews our attitudes toward God and changes our lives in the strangest way. He constantly and unyieldingly uses his divine law to kill our sinful selves in order to make us alive in Christ through his gospel (Romans 7:9-12; 8:1-4). Death is necessary for life, as Jesus' death on our behalf clearly demonstrates. The changeover from bondage to the law of sin and death to the fresh way of life in God is not our achievement (Romans chapters 6–8). God's Spirit works a change in our hearts through his holy and powerful Word (Acts 2:36-39). Without Christ, repentance only leads to despair (Matthew 27:3-5; 2 Corinthians 7:10). With Christ, it is the narrow door to life with God (Matthew 7:14; Acts 2:36-39). What does this mean?

Keys to the festival door

The way to God is not paved with mere sorrow for wrongdoings or even terrors of conscience. Self-induced remorse is at best partial or fragmentary. Like sorrow over actual wrongdoings, it cannot cover all bases or get to the root of the problem. But true repentance consists of godly sorrow over sin and faith in God's mercy (Luke 24:47; Isaiah 30:15; 2 Corinthians 7:10). Because true repentance is rooted in and based on Christ and his redeeming work, it covers our entire lives and is as certain as Christ's death for the world's sins. In godly sorrow we need not recall each and every sin, weighing, distinguishing, and differentiating one from another. This turns confession into torture. It is enough to confess that we are altogether sinful from birth and to admit that we sin against God in thoughts, words, and deeds as mirrored in God's law (Psalm 51:1-5). In this way we confess all sins without omitting or forgetting a single one (Psalm 19:12).

In this way also, sorrow over sin and faith in God encompass our entire lives constantly and consistently, whether we are waking or sleeping—and continue until we die. In this way we have a whole new outlook toward God, toward life, toward the world, and toward our neighbors. As a result we no longer live for ourselves alone but in Christ and for our neighbor (Colossians 3:1-3,12-14). We live in Christ by faith and for our neighbor by love. God alone works this new way of life in our lives through his Word and sacrament.

In simple terms, God comes to our rescue. His strength is made perfect in our weakness (2 Corinthians 12:9,10). The almighty God invites us to come to his side and calls us to repentance (Acts 2:38,39; Genesis 17:1,2; John 15:26). Repentance (meta-noia) basically is God-centered.

God aims to bring about a major change in us—a change in the direction of our lives, a change in lifestyle, a change (*meta*) of mind and attitude (*nous*), a new life of faith. God is the active doer and we are the unworthy recipients of his Word and work.

Through his law God constantly makes us aware of our sinful shortcomings (Romans 3:23). Through his gospel he consistently creates a whole new mindset and strengthens our faith in him (Romans 8:1-11; 1 Corinthians 2:12-16). For this reason God uses the Lord's Supper as a powerful visual and earthly means to strengthen the bond of faith. The Lord of the Supper purposefully summons the downcast to eat bread and wine from his table. He wants to fill the hungry with good gifts, give us the comfort of his presence, and bless us with his forgiveness and rest.

The invitation to the Lord's Supper, therefore, includes all who trust Jesus when he says, "This is my body . . . for many for the forgiveness of sins." With outstretched hands, open mouths, and repentant hearts, banquet celebrants receive the Word of Life as an inheritance from God. In his name Jesus absolves us from all guilt and through his blood releases us from slavery to sin, the law, and death (Romans chapters 6–8). God's mercy and compassion alone cause our hearts to break for joy and prevent us from taking the Lord's invitation and his meal lightly. But the warning against hypocrisy at the table still stands for good reason. God gives us a caution card lest we sin against the Lord's body and blood in ignorance or eat in lighthearted unconcern—and so partake of his meal not to our joy but to our judgment (1 Corinthians 11:27-29).

Even before his ascension, Jesus took measures to guard the festal door as securely as he safeguarded the gate to paradise in Eden (Luke 13:23-30; 13:34; Genesis 3:21-24).

Anticipating his death, Jesus gave his followers keys to the kingdom of heaven and placed into their hands the passport to paradise (Matthew 16:19; John 20:23). He asks his followers to make known this simple truth: The door to life with God stands open for the penitent and downcast but is closed to despisers and doubters.

This key action is meant especially to comfort anxious sinners but, at the same time, it posts a warning not to persist in sin or unbelief. Closing the banquet door to manifestly impenitent people is not the loveless act it appears to be. Locking the door is as critical a call to repentance as is leaving the door open (Matthew 18:15-20; Hebrews 3:12-15). Closing the door to celebrating Communion with God is a stern reminder to forsake a godless way of life and turn to God in sincere sorrow (1 Corinthians 5:1-5). The same set of keys that closes the door to God's banquet hall also opens it again for all who trust his mercy and forgiveness.

The Lord's concern for our welfare is the chief reason why all who come to the table need to know and understand what is happening at the Supper (1 Corinthians 11:27-29). The Lamb's high feast is not a mere sociological phenomenon, religious get-together, friendly handshake among peoples, or spiritual potluck. As engaging as such social interaction appears on the surface, it short-circuits the work of Christ. God's ways are not our ways (Isaiah 55:6-8). Life with God is life from God. Rooted in Christ, faith is proven true by deeds of love and charity as we interact daily in our community and country.

To understand God's ways, we have a clear example in Abraham, the father of believers (Galatians 3:6-9). This Aramean nomad, patriarch of the Jews and father of the Arabs, is a primary teacher of Christian faith (Genesis

12:1-5). His biography answers with unmatched clarity the questions of the ages: How do we stand before God? Do we gain God's favor as a reward for service performed? Or do we stand before God by faith in what God has done for us (Romans 4:1-13)?

The reward-for-service model is fundamental to human relationships in our world. We get a reward in return for what we do. Workers receive wages as an obligation, not a gift. They earn it. Does this same ideal hold true with God? Does he owe us something because of what we have done for him? The life of Abraham, the father of believers, tells us otherwise (Galatians 3:1-9). God directed his life by promises. He promised this wandering nomad possession of a new land and this childless couple a large family for a special reason. From Abraham's land and lineage a descendant was to come. This offspring was to be a special blessing and Savior of the world (Genesis 15:1-21).

And Abraham believed God—sight unseen! He followed God's Word, left family and friends behind, settled in a strange land appointed by God, and waited for God's direction. Abraham's hope for the future rested on one thing alone—God's promise (Hebrews 11:1,8-19). Consequently, the Scriptures repeatedly record that "Abraham *believed* the LORD, and he credited it to him as righteousness" (Genesis 15:6; Romans 4:3; Galatians 3:6; James 2:23). In one woman's words, "It's so clear and simple. Why haven't I heard this before?"

Approaching the Lord's Table

How then do we stand before God, come into God's presence, and approach the Lord's Table? The answer in a nutshell is found in Jesus—Abraham's direct descendant, child of Mary, offspring of King David's line, Messiah of the

Jews, and Savior of humankind. He is the Lamb of God, prefigured in Israel's sacrifices and prophesied in patriarchal promises (Deuteronomy 18:15; 2 Samuel 7:11-16; Isaiah 7:13,14; John 1:29-34). God's answer to the all-important question of life is revealed openly in Jesus. Abraham's greater Son is God's promised Son whose mission to humankind climaxed on the cross (Philippians 2:6-8).

The cross is God's judgment on the world. With the death of his Son on the cross, God the Father pronounced sentence on sinful life with absolute finality (John 19:30). He laid on Jesus the sins of the world (Isaiah 53:6; Luke 22:39-44). On the altar of the cross, God's sacrificial Lamb ended the rule of sin and death forever. At the death of Jesus, God's holiness and righteousness met in a miracle of divine mercy.

No wonder Paul was determined to preach nothing "except Jesus Christ and him crucified" (1 Corinthians 2:2). Jesus' crucifixion unlocks our understanding of God's Word and explains our invitation to the Sacrament. The cross reveals two things simultaneously: God's anger over sin and his love for us sinners. The proclamation of Christ's death is an earnest advertisement both of God's righteous anger and his forgiving love. At the crucifixion God's law and gospel embrace in an act of divine reconciliation and bring us to our knees in faith and hope. The Lamb who died on the cross is our Savior (Revelation 22:12-16; 1 Corinthians 2:8-10).

To know God, therefore, is to know how law and gospel encapsulate God's ways in perfect harmony. The two teachings reveal what we might call the two faces of God. The law is God's holy face. It frowns on all that is not pure and perfect in his sight and requires obedience that we cannot muster on our own. The law shows us our sins as clearly as a mirror reflects our image and reveals how deep the gap is between God's way of life and ours.

The gospel is God's loving face. It shines on us with gracious forgiveness (Numbers 6:24-26). In the gospel God bends down to us in love, touches our lives, and gives what we are unable to achieve by nature (Romans 5:15-17). The gospel comforts consciences shaken by life's bitter experiences and makes death a day of victory (1 Corinthians 15:50-57).

Now we can look at life and God in a whole different light and listen to his Word in an entirely different way. This new way is the hearing of faith, a new obedience to God that comes by faith (Romans 10:17-21; Galatians 3:2). In thanksgiving we sing a new song, as fresh and new as God's new covenant. The song of God's love is not a sad song. It is a song of thanks for deliverance and a bold confidence in facing the future (Revelation 5:9,10; Exodus 15:1-18; Psalm 96; 149). In view of God's mercy, it is our turn to give. We now offer our bodies as living sacrifices, holy and pleasing to God, and give our lives in works of service to church and community (Romans 12:1-21). In effect we become "little christs" to our neighbors—bending in love to our neighbors' weaknesses and helping them in times of need. In this way others come to know how God's love and Christ's work are the sources of our strength (Matthew 25:34-40). As it was in paradise, we reflect God's image once again, approach his table to eat the fruit of the tree of life, and celebrate our lives with God.

Sad to say, despisers of God's Word and ways exclude themselves from this joyous celebration. True to form, God's opponents unmask hidden attitudes by outward acts and words. Yet no measure of opposition is able to negate God's love for us. Neither faith nor unbelief can ever invalidate God's love for one primary reason. God never changes. As Lord, he stands firm in his sovereign ways (James 1:16-18). God is love. We do not create God or his nature. We do not mandate God's love for his creation (1 John 4:7-10).

But by our nature we can deceive. To all appearances we can profess to be spiritual and religious. Yet without God's love in Christ, we are nothing but pious frauds— outwardly reveling in spirituality but inwardly coddling a dead faith. Hypocrites and deceivers cannot act in union with God (James 1:26,27; 1 John 4:1-6). Wrapped in the cloak of self-righteousness, spiritually self-centered people prefer to play God and make unlovely judgments on other people (Luke 18:9-14). Such religious enthusiasts parade their lives before God without confessing their unworthiness, without being heart-struck by God's condemnation of all self-righteousness, without calling to God for mercy.

We know hypocrisy well. Its description fits all of us by nature and points to the need for daily contrition and repentance. The life of faith is not an easy thing. And no one knows the strength of faith unless one is tested and tried (Matthew 4:1-11). To approach God's table while patently persisting in a self-righteous and unholy lifestyle calls down God's judgment on life. God is never neutral in his divine judgments. He comes to save or to condemn. God sent his Son to judge the world in righteousness and truth. Christ's concern is always *for* us (John 3:16-21). But those who are against him in unbelief and impenitence are already self-condemned (Matthew 12:30-32).

For good reason, therefore, the Lord asks us to exclude from his table those who manifestly persist in sin despite warnings. This earnest and loving action is God's way of caring and is a call to a whole new attitude toward him and his creation. All who excuse from the Lord's banquet, hesitate to confess their wrongs, or doubt Jesus' words lose out on the great blessing he announces, "Take and eat; this is my body. . . . Drink. . . . This is my blood . . . poured out for many for the forgiveness of sins."

United in Christ

Now we know how extremely important it is to recognize God's ways in his Holy Word and Supper (1 Corinthians 11:27-29). Understanding God's ways always has to do with God's Word. God does not deal with us in the abstract. He deals with us in concrete, lifelike, vivid, and expressive images. He comes to us visibly and intimately in the person of Jesus Christ, who is "the *image* of the invisible God." Jesus' mission is to restore God's image to us (Genesis 1:27; 5:3; Colossians 1:15). God sent Jesus to return the life that was originally lost through Adam's sinful break with God. The breakthrough to a new life with God comes through Jesus as the second Adam (Romans 5:15). When approached by Jesus, we can tell others about him as pointedly and excitely as did Jesus' first disciples: "We have found the one . . . Jesus of Nazareth" (John 1:43-50).

This simple witness to Jesus does not use abstract but historical images. It speaks about a real-life person. It deals with a *mystery* now fully revealed in Jesus Christ (Colossians 1:26). Even today, as in bygone days, we sing the good news of Jesus with the same clear images as in the hymn of the early church: "The mystery of godliness is great: He appeared in a body, was vindicated by the Spirit, was seen by angels, was preached among the nations, was believed on in the world, was taken up in glory" (1 Timothy 3:16).

We receive God's benefits in the same images as did Paul in explaining the Lord's Supper to Christian congregations: "Is not the cup of thanksgiving for which we give thanks a participation in the blood of Christ? And is not the bread that we break a participation in the body of Christ? Because there is one loaf, we, who are many, are one body, for we all partake of the one loaf" (1 Corinthians 10:16,17). So the mysteries of God touch our lives, and the image of Christ colors our relations to God and one another. To embrace this relationship, we return to the past.

A mystical union

Since the beginning of human life in Eden, no image projects our union with God in a more stark and natural way than the image of birthing and marriage. A single command of God to our original parents signaled the generation of human life in God's creation. To Adam and Eve—that is, to the Earthling (Adam) and Life (Eve), to man and woman, to male and female, to human beings both—God gave his creative Word by a dynamic command: "Be fruitful and increase in number; fill the earth and subdue it" (Genesis 1:28). This creative Word from God has to do with life's beginnings and its continuation, with the gift of earthly life and the intimacy of marriage, with sex and family.

What God commands, he fulfills. He empowers us to do what he commands. He establishes the marriage union to carry out his divine will in an ongoing and orderly way. The history of human life is a familiar story: "A man will leave his father and mother and be united to his wife, and they will become one flesh" (Genesis 2:24). Through the union of the two sexes in marriage, God acts to fill the earth with people, to honor the intimacy of marriage, and to bring glory to himself (1 Corinthians 11:11,12).

The images of birthing and marriage also mirror and echo God's relationship to us in the church (Ephesians 5:31,32). Since Eden, births and weddings are God's expressions used to proclaim union and reconciliation with God. No image is more stark, more natural, or more real to depict God and us in the new life of faith than the one implanted in God's creative order. None brings the emotions of faith to the fore more intimately and intensely. The bridegroom/bride relationship, anchored in human life and sexuality, is so strong and vivid an image that it brings joy to the hearts of believers. It evokes a happiness that takes Christians captive and anticipates a final reunion with God at death (Revelation 21:9,10,23-27).

The bridal image is central to understanding Christ's work on earth and his gift in the Lord's Supper. Christian life has its setting in the work of Christ as the heavenly Bridegroom. The bride/Bridegroom image opens for us the unbelievable paradox of life. It explains how sinners become saints through union with Jesus. It reveals how a righteous God forgives our wrongs, sets aside his anger, and freely declares his love for us once more (Hosea 14:1-4; Song of Songs 4:1; Isaiah 44:2). It clarifies how the mystery of God's work on earth is grasped by faith alone. How is this done?

This bride/bridegroom relationship proclaims the *joyous exchange* between bride and bridegroom in powerful scriptural imagery. This image describes how faith unites us with Christ as a bride is united with her Bridegroom. By this mystery, as a Christian teacher once observed, Christ becomes one flesh with us in a true marriage (Ephesians 5:25-32). It is the most perfect of all marriages, of which human marriages are only poor examples. In this union with Christ, we hold everything in common. What Christ has we have as if it were our own. And what we have Christ claims as if it were his own.

To grasp this *mystical union* is to comprehend the inestimable benefits of faith. Christ is full of grace, life, and salvation. We are full of sins, death, and damnation. In this marriage we are united with Christ by the bond of faith. As our Bridegroom, Jesus must take on himself the things that are his bride's and, in exchange, give his bride the things that are his. If he gives her his body and very self, why should he not give her all that is his? And if he takes the body of the bride, why should he not take all that is hers? So our heavenly Bridegroom takes our sins, death, and damnation as his dowry. And his grace, life, and salvation become our possession.

This most *joyous exchange* is not only about a mystical union with Christ. It is also about sharing Christ's holy struggle and victory, his salvation and redemption. Our Bridegroom is God and man in one person. As God he cannot sin, die, or be condemned. His righteousness, life, and salvation are unconquerable, eternal, and omnipotent. And yet by the *wedding ring of faith* he shares in the sins, death, and pains of hell that are his bride's. He makes them his own and acts as though they were his own, as if he himself had sinned. He suffered, died, and was buried to overcome them all.

Since Christ is a heavenly Bridegroom, his righteousness is greater than the sins of all people, his life is stronger than death, and his salvation is more invincible than hell. So by the pledge of faith his bride is free in Christ, her Bridegroom—free from all sins and secure against death and hell. As the bride, she receives eternal righteousness, life, and salvation as a dowry from her

Bridegroom, Christ. In this glorious union, he takes to himself a glorious bride, without spot or wrinkle. She is his by faith in the Word of Life, righteousness, and salvation (Ephesians 5:26,27). In this way he marries her in faith and steadfast love and betroths her in mercy, righteousness, and justice (Hosea 2:19,20).

Who can fully appreciate what this royal marriage means? Who can understand the riches of God's grace? This rich and divine Bridegroom marries this poor, wicked harlot, redeems her from all her evil, and adorns her with all his goodness. Her sins can no longer haunt or destroy her because they are laid upon Christ and swallowed up by him. In Christ, her husband, she has a righteousness to boast of as her own—a righteousness that she can boldly display alongside her sins when faced with death and hell. She can say with wedded bliss and confidence, "I have sinned, yet my Christ, to whom I am pledged by faith, has not sinned. And all that is his is mine and all that is mine is his." As the bride in the Song of Solomon says, "My lover is mine and I am his" (Song of Songs 2:16).

The image of union with Christ helps us understand not merely how much is ascribed to faith in Christ but also that we stand before God just and holy only by faith in Christ. Justification by faith alone is not a doctrine "colder than ice" as some charge. The bridal image embodies the rapturous exchange between Christ and sinners in a dynamic way. It fills the heart of the bride with joy in life and certainty for life everlasting. Earthly marriages are reserved for this life; our union with Christ lasts forever. When the Lord gives us his body and blood to strengthen the bond of faith with him and all believers, his Supper serves its purpose.

Fellowship with the Lamb

As host at the Supper, therefore, Jesus is not inviting us to a simple get-together at a spiritual kitchen. At the Last Supper before his death, he put the Lamb's high feast on high priority, explicitly saying, "I tell you, I will not drink of this fruit of the vine from now on until that day when I drink it anew with you in my Father's kingdom" (Matthew 26:29). In this way Jesus refocuses our attention, breaks the barriers of time and space, and sets his banquet under the guise of eternity.

At the banquet table, Jesus anticipates that he will first drink the cup of God's judgment alone for a reason. His death will bring about new life in God's kingdom. Jesus eats the last meal with his disciples to prepare them for new life with their Father in heaven. On the memorial day of the old covenant, Jesus establishes the new covenant for the new age. Once the Lamb's perfect sacrifice is carried out on the cross, Passover meals cease to function. Those who eat the banquet meal "from now on" renew fellowship with God that lasts indefinitely for time immemorial. How is this done?

At the Supper, Christ indicates that we receive God's antidote for death and dying. Eating the Lord's Supper certifies that someday our bodies will break death's bonds and rise to life just as our Savior did. On that day we too will break the time barrier of here and now and will from then on live in God's kingdom forever. We who now eat with the Lamb on earth will also eat in God's house in unbroken fellowship with all God's people (Isaiah 25:6-8; Luke 14:15-24; Revelation 19:9).

Celebrating the Lamb's high feast on earth, therefore, is a foretaste of future life in God's kingdom. Already now scattered saints on earth share this inheritance with gathered saints in heaven (Revelation 5:6-14). Union with Christ now and reunion with God then gives us a unity that members of Christ's body share forever (1 John 3:1-3). In a graphic double picture, the apostle Paul tells believers how those who eat Christ's body are already one body in Christ here and now. "Because there is one loaf," he writes with simple words and descriptive insight, "we, who are many, are one body, for we all partake of the one loaf" (1 Corinthians 10:17).

Communion of saints

Even though believers are many by count, they are really only one body. Christian unity comes alone through Jesus and his work (Ephesians 4:1-16). In confessing faith in Christ, believers call Christ's church the communion of saints for good reason. *Communion* is the word for what we hold in common and refers both to Christ's church and to his Supper. Christians are one body in Christ simply because they have one Lord and eat of the one loaf.

But, true to form, the communion of saints remains *concealed* under the cross. Hidden in a crowd of people, the church is present wherever Christ's Word of forgiveness is proclaimed, offered, guaranteed, and believed. There the Father establishes his kingdom in the hearts of believers; the seed takes root in earth's soil (Luke 17:20,21; 8:4-15). Yet only those who truly trust God's Word are the communion of saints and derive benefit from eating at the Lamb's high feast. Hidden beneath the veil of persecution, sufferings, outward divisions, and false teachings, God's kingdom is nevertheless established on earth to prepare us for the kingdom of glory in heaven (Matthew 6:9,10).

So the forgiveness that Christ offers to us individually in his Supper we share with a host of saints. The common bond of God's love unites believers worldwide in the body of Christ. Those united to Christ by faith are united through Christ to one another. The Sacrament of Holy Communion is God's way of visibly guaranteeing life with God and unites God's saints in common faith. Faith in Jesus' work and Word alone brings about the blessed unity that Christ asks his Father to preserve (John 17:11-17).

For this reason it is vital to come to God's Table knowing what the Supper is all about and recognizing its purpose (1 Corinthians 11:28). Christians at Corinth needed to learn that lesson—and we need to learn from them. At Corinth, participants in the meal understood the feast superficially. Many remained self-centered in their attitudes and cared less about the welfare of others. As a result, the fellowship of faith fragmented. How did such confusion come about?

The Corinthian church incorporated the Lord's Supper into its gatherings, which included regular daily meals (1 Corinthians 11:17-33). Wealthy people brought food for the poor. In Christian tradition, the congregation undoubtedly called on God to bless its daily bread and, at the same time, did not forget the last meal that Jesus ate before his death. In Christian piety, the congregation called this combination mealtime/Lord's Supper an *agape* meal or love feast.

But habits at the common meals belied the unity and fellowship they held as Christians. Sharing and caring for one another gave way to satisfying personal hunger and thirst. Some overate and even got drunk; others went away hungry from the love feast. Loveless action made a mockery of celebrating the Lord's Supper. Many actually ate and drank God's judgment on themselves in unbelief and unconcern. Such divisive behavior broke the congregation's unity.

The congregation evidently needed instruction regarding the Lord's Supper. And the apostle Paul obliged. He carefully taught the congregation by letter and explicitly explained how the Lord's meal fit into Christian life. He wanted the members to realize that eating the body and blood of Christ at Christ's meal also affects the church as the body of Christ. Christ's Supper is not eaten merely for the moment but is celebrated for one's eternal welfare. In their undisciplined and selfish eating, some members were sinning against the body and blood of the Lord. By their behavior, they were undoing the purpose for which Christ suffered, died, and rose from death.

Paul, therefore, gave Christians the big picture in simple terms. He first repeated the words that the Lord Jesus spoke at the time he instituted the meal (1 Corinthians 11:23-25). Then he put these words into perspective by pointing to the Lord's coming. Just as Jesus did at the Last Supper, the apostle projected the use of the Supper from time into eternity. "For whenever you eat this bread and drink this cup," Paul stated with careful instruction, "you proclaim the Lord's death *until he comes*" (1 Corinthians 11:26).

To celebrate life with God is to recognize that Christ did not die to foster sin, bring about death, coddle our fleshly desires, or give in to evil, as the examples of some Christians seem to indicate (1 Corinthians 11:27-32; Galatians 2:17-21). Impenitent behavior has no place at the Lamb's high feast. It defeats the reason for Christ's invitation to celebrate life with God. No, the Lord's Supper proclaims Christ's death on the cross to break sin's rule over our life, to conquer death that separates us from God, and to hail his victory over Satan, the arch-deceiver.

At the Lamb's high feast

The Lord's Supper, therefore, uniquely joins the present promise of forgiveness with a future promise of life in God's kingdom. It sets our eyes on the end of time, according to Jesus' engaging words, "I will come back" (John 14:2,3; Acts 1:11). Jesus' final appearance on earth marks the day of judgment and fulfills God's aim to gather all things to himself in Christ. The waiting church on earth proclaims, "Come, O Lord!" (*maranatha* in Jesus' tongue) and lives in anxious expectation of the day. It celebrates its life with God in the Holy Supper of the Lord with unending thanksgiving (*eucharist*) (1 Corinthians 16:22; 1 Thessalonians 3:13; 4:15; Revelation 22:20).

On that day Christ will fulfill his promise: "I tell you, I will not drink of this fruit of the vine from now on until that day when I drink it anew with you in my Father's kingdom" (Matthew 26:29). Every Christian who eats the meal now anticipates the end of time. The invitation to eat and drink at the table of the Lord points us to the certain future with God secured by Jesus' death. The proclamation of his death continues in each successive meal until Christ's arrival.

On the Last Day, the church on earth joins the church in heaven in receiving its final benediction: "Blessed are those who are invited to the wedding supper of the Lamb!" (Revelation 19:9). The scene, in John's graphic description, is the vision of faith fulfilled. At the throne of God, what is hidden now under the seal of God's revelation will then be open to clear view (Revelation 5:1-14). The One worthy to break the seal is none other than Jesus—the victorious Messiah, the Lion of Judah of Jewish origin from the root of David. He is the Lamb who stands at the place of honor at the center of God's throne. He appears as the victim but is now the victor. And all creation and the church encircle the victor who possesses full power and the sevenfold energy of God's Spirit (Revelation 1:4; Isaiah 11:2).

The Lamb takes the sealed record from God's right hand and opens it. And all creation and the church—his beneficiaries—fall down in homage to the Lamb that was slain. A prayer of praise and thanks accompanies the church's new song of deliverance. The Lamb is worthy of such thanksgiving . . . because as our vicar, he died . . . because as the victim, his lifeblood redeems people from every tribe, language, people, and nation . . . because as victor, he makes the church to rule with him.

Angels in infinite numbers join all creation and the church in singing aloud a grand "Te Deum" in worship of Christ, the Lamb Redeemer:

> "Worthy is the Lamb, who was slain,
> to receive power and wealth and wisdom and strength
> and honor and glory and praise!" (Revelation 5:12)

They address the song to the Lamb who was slain for a special reason. He alone is worthy to receive our praise because only he fully possesses those sevenfold attributes that belong to God alone.

An echo chorus joins in the new song. All that has life and breath in heaven, on earth, under the earth, and on the sea join together in a final grand chorus of thanksgiving to God enthroned on high and to the Lamb Redeemer. To this all creation says, "Amen," and the church worships its Lord with all due reverence.

This glorious vision of the future comes to us hidden under the form of bread and wine. At the Lord's Supper, Jesus is present. The Lamb that was slain for us says to us in all simplicity: *"Take and eat; this is my body, which is given for you. Do this in remembrance of me."* And *"Drink from it, all of you; this is my blood of the new covenant, which is poured out for you for the forgiveness of sins. Do this, whenever you drink it, in remembrance of me."*

The Lamb's high feast is set for us, dear reader. Every day globally, in languages strange to one another, people from every nation communicate in these simple words. As they receive the Lord's Supper, they eat and drink in common. This festive meal is, as it was meant to be, God's people sharing God's gift of forgiveness until he comes. Until that day, we celebrate life each day by faith in Christ and serve him and his world in thanksgiving.

> Jesus, Lord of life, I pray you,
> Let me gladly here obey you.
> By your love I am invited;
> Be your love with love requited.
> By this supper let me measure,
> Lord, how vast and deep love's treasure.
> Through the gift of grace you give me
> As your guest in heav'n receive me. (CW 311:8)

Appendix 1—
Luther's Small Catechism

The Institution of Holy Communion

First: *What is the Sacrament of Holy Communion?*

It is the true body and blood of our Lord Jesus Christ under the bread and wine, instituted by Christ for us Christians to eat and to drink.

Where is this written?

The holy evangelists Matthew, Mark, Luke, and the apostle Paul tell us: Our Lord Jesus Christ, on the night he was betrayed, took bread; and when he had given thanks, he broke it and gave it to his disciples, saying, "Take and eat; this is my body, which is given for you. Do this in remembrance of me."

Then he took the cup, gave thanks, and gave it to them, saying, "Drink from it, all of you; this is my blood of the new covenant, which is poured out for you for the forgiveness of sins. Do this, whenever you drink it, in remembrance of me."

The Blessings of Holy Communion

Second: *What blessing do we receive through this eating and drinking?*

That is shown us by these words: "Given" and "poured out for you for the forgiveness of sins." Through these words we receive forgiveness of sins, life, and salvation in this sacrament.

For where there is forgiveness of sins, there is also life and salvation.

The Power of Holy Communion

Third: *How can eating and drinking do such great things?*

It is certainly not the eating and drinking that does such things, but the words "Given" and "poured out for you for the forgiveness of sins."

These words are the main thing in this sacrament, along with the eating and drinking.

And whoever believes these words has what they plainly say, the forgiveness of sins.

The Reception of Holy Communion

Fourth: *Who, then, is properly prepared to receive this sacrament?*

Fasting and other outward preparations may serve a good purpose, but he is properly prepared who believes these words: "Given" and "poured out for you for the forgiveness of sins."

But whoever does not believe these words or doubts them is not prepared, because the words "for you" require nothing but hearts that believe.

Appendix 2—
The Augsburg Confession of 1530
(from the German text)

Article X: The Holy Supper of Our Lord
It is taught among us that the true body and blood of Christ are really present in the Supper of our Lord under the form of bread and wine and are there distributed and received. The contrary doctrine is therefore rejected.

Article XIII: The Use of the Sacraments
It is taught among us that the sacraments were instituted not only to be signs by which people might be identified outwardly as Christians, but that they are signs and testimonies of God's will toward us for the purpose of awakening and strengthening our faith. For this reason they require faith, and they are rightly used when they are received in faith and for the purpose of strengthening faith.

For Further Reading

The Book of Concord

Augsburg Confession: Article XXII: Both Kinds in the Sacrament; Article XXIV: The Mass.

Apology of the Augsburg Confession: Article X: The Holy Supper; Article XXII: The Lord's Supper under Both Kinds; Article XXIV: The Mass.

Smalcald Articles: Part III, VI: The Sacrament of the Altar.

Formula of Concord, Epitome: Article VII: The Holy Supper of Christ.

Formula of Concord, Solid Declaration: Article VII: The Holy Supper.

Brug, John, *Church Fellowship: Working Together for the Truth*. Milwaukee: Northwestern Publishing House, 1996. This book treats the topic of church fellowship as the scriptural principles of fellowship apply to the practice of closed Communion.

Essays in *Our Great Heritage*, 3 vols. Edited by Lyle W. Lange. Milwaukee: Northwestern Publishing House, 1991:

Habeck, Irwin. "Who May Officiate at the Lord's Supper?" Vol. 3.

Koelpin, Arnold. "The Sacramental Presence in the Theology of the Synodical Conference." Vol. 3.

Kretzmann, Paul. "Admission to, and Registration for, the Lord's Supper." Vol. 3.

Hoenecke, Adolph. *Evangelical Lutheran Dogmatics*, Volume IV. Milwaukee: Northwestern Publishing House, 1999: "The Lord's Supper," 105-151.

"Statement on the Lord's Supper." *Doctrinal Statements of the WELS*. Milwaukee: Northwestern Publishing House, 1997: 57-60.

WELS Web site www.wels.net, Questions + Answers. Here one can find answers to many practical questions about the Lord's Supper.

Scripture Index

Subject Index